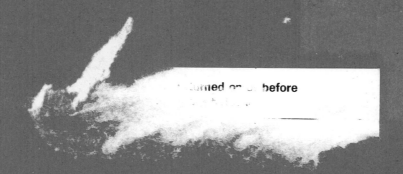

Zandra Rhodes

a lifelong love affair with textiles

This edition published in 2005 by the Antique Collectors' Club Ltd. and
Zandra Rhodes Publications Limited

First published 2005
Copyright © 2005 by Zandra Rhodes
World Copyright Reserved

Gity Monsef, Dennis Nothdruft and Robert de Niet assert their moral right to be identified as the
authors of this book. Edited by Ben Scholten and Madeleine Ginsburg.

Every effort has been made to obtain all necessary permissions to reproduce images.
Any errors or omissions should be notified to the publisher and will be corrected in later editions.

British Library Cataloguing-in-Publication Date

A CIP catalogue record for the book is available from the British Library.

ISBN 1 85149 486 3 (Paperback)
ISBN 1 85149 484 7 (Hardback)

Cover photograph by Piers Atkinson
Back cover by Simon Wheeler
FTM photography by Robyn Beeche
Art direction and design by Robert de Niet

Type set in Interstate

Printed and Bound in Spain for
Antique Collectors' Club Ltd, Sandy Lane, Old Martlesham, Woodbridge, Suffolk, IP12 4SD

Zandra Rhodes Publications Limited, 1 Minster Court, Tuscam Way, Camberley, Surrey, GU15 3YY

Zandra Rhodes

a lifelong love affair with textiles

Fashion and Textile Museum

Antique Collectors' Club

4

This catalogue is dedicated to Salah Hassanein who has enabled me to achieve my dream of the Fashion & Textile Museum against all obstacles

My special thanks are also due to the following FTM Friends and the American Friends of the Zandra Rhodes Museum who by their special contributions enabled the publication of this catalogue:

Audrey S. Geisel, Dr Seuss Enterprises
Sheri Jamieson
Jeannie Jones
Luis da Silva

backstage
photograph by
Clive Arrowsmith,
model Nell Campell and
Leonard of London, 1977

acknowledgments

I would like to thank all my friends for their support in helping me achieve this catalogue and encouraging me to do this retrospective exhibition of my work. Especially David Sassoon who, apart from being a great designer in his own right, is a Museum Trustee, supporting the Fashion and Textile Museum with its exhibits, and is always coming up with new ideas. Thanks also to Sophie Hamilton, our Chairperson, and our other trustees: especially Mark Jones and Patrick Boylan for their invaluable help and advice and Bruce Galbraith for believing in the Museum.

I am particularly grateful to all those photographers who immediately said yes to allowing me to use their photographs and enable me to capture the atmosphere of my dresses in their period context. Especially Robyn Beeche, assisted by Jason Smith, for photographing all the exhibition garments and Kevin Arpino for organising the loan of the beautiful Adel Rootstein mannequins. A special thank you to Michael Southgate who enabled me to find special mannequin parts to do the photographs. Another special thank you to Condé Nast for agreeing to allow me to use their Vogue pictures and likewise the Norman Parkinson Estate. Brenda Polan for writing the lead essay and enabling FTM to work with Surrey College of Art; thank you to Robert de Niet who painstakingly worked to design and set up this catalogue and prepared it for printing, assisted by Audrey Barrett, Rob Hare, Laura Jones, Kev Speck. Together with Gity Monsef, my Creative Director, who painstakingly went through the extensive pictorial archives to find the pictures and who believed and fought for this project; and Dennis Nothdruft for writing the exhibition introductions. Jennifer Donaghy, Elena Grasset and Jill McGregor for typing and chasing up photographic permissions; Kaye Newman, Course Coordinator of the Cass Graduate Design Consultancy division of London Metropolitan University, for teaming with the FTM and allowing Thomas Gilbey to scan and prepare the photographic images; our students, Alison Hakes, Andrea Keene, Kara O'Connell, Rose Sullivan and Gemma Winter who worked tirelessly to do background organisation; Madeleine Ginsburg for her valued consultation, help and always being there for us.

Zandra Rhodes staff, especially Frances Diplock for organising, revamping, and preparing the dresses for photography and Ben Scholten, who designs the collection with me, for reviewing everything to ensure it is in order and is correct. Martin Tollhurst and staff, Diane Gowland and David Reeson of Newham College of Further Education, for believing in and partnering with the Fashion and Textile Museum to create the Learning Centre without which our computer work would not have been possible. Gabi Longhi Chautin for taking on the task of chasing the testimonials from April Ashley, Manolo Blahnik, Simon Doonan, Britt Ekland, Brian Eno, Joseph Ettegui, Kaffe Fassett, Sir Christopher Frayling, Larry & Maj Hagman, Anjelica Huston, Fredericka Hunter, Jenny Kee, Christian Lacroix, Barry Lategan, Andrew Logan, Marylou Luther, Issey Miyake, Mary Quant, Joan Agajanian Quinn, David Sassoon, Vidal Sassoon, Sandy Schreier, Jane Shepherdson, Cameron Silver, Maxine Smith and Mario Testino. My Californian staff: Takayo Kawaguchi who painstakingly typed my notes and Chetna Bhatt who scanned and prepared additional pictures; my American Friends Chairperson, Patricia O'Connor, who has helped me fundraise to achieve this catalogue.

Thank you to Michael Howells who designed the exhibition for the museum.

Finally thanks to Salah Hassanein who has enabled me to put together this exhibition and also this catalogue.

Dec 2004

contents

ZandraRhodes

a lifelong love affair with textiles

foreword
by Gity Monsef
Creative Director
Fashion and Textile Museum

The work of Zandra Rhodes spans more than thirty-years and represents a love affair with colour and print. The three thousand original garments she has kept in her archive, along with sketchbooks, paperwork and drawings illustrates every part of her design process: from original sketches, to kodatrace, to screen print, to garment. It is a work resource, still in continuous use, and a unique reservoir of design experience for students and for all who love fashion. Zandra Rhodes is still at heart a creative artist, whose work is a reflection of a generation that has lived through a period of seismic change: economic, social and artistic.

The archive is on loan to the Fashion and Textile Museum, which gives us a unique opportunity to provide a multi-layered experience of the essential and basic relationship between fashion and design. Textile archives abound, but it is rare to find one of such completeness and this was significant in persuading Zandra Rhodes to found the museum in the first place. It is not, as so often in museums, a secondary source of study, but a live and a prime one for possibly the oldest, as well as the most perishable, of the applied arts.

It is also valuable on another level, in featuring designs of the 1970s and 1980s that are a tours de force of colour, change and form. As an opportunity of seeing more of what is perhaps the richest and most inspirational period of British fashion, it is yet another live and lively reference for many of the young designers today.

This first British retrospective of Zandra Rhodes provides us with the creative inspiration, the technical background and experience that inform every single item on show. From the beginning of her career, Zandra Rhodes has challenged fashion conventions and led the way in experimenting with fabric. With no formal training in fashion design she has a maverick approach. The first designer to allow the print to dictate the shape of the garment, she was also the first to use seams on the outside of the garments and the first to make dresses with carefully tailored tears held together with safety pins.

This exhibition and accompanying catalogue explore the various themes behind the Zandra Rhodes vision, using examples of her early work, which changed the way we look at the relationship of clothing and textile design. The Dinosaur Coat, the Lily Collection, Conceptual Chic, Mediaeval Collections, the rarely seen Spanish Impressions and the Chinese Collection are all examples of her unique contribution.

The exhibition is divided into seven sections: *The Process*, *The Shape*, *Colour*, *Technique*, *The Dress*, *One World* and, finally, *The Woman*. These sections represent her most important contributions to the fashion world.

We begin with *The Process*, which gives us an insight in to the thought processes behind her work. This is a "behind the scenes" look at all the elements involved in creating a Zandra Rhodes garment: the inspirational research, photographs and objects, initial sketches and prints in various colourways. It is also a step-by-step analysis of the various stages that go into the creation of the textile and the final garment.

The Shape is one of the most important factors behind the style. For her, the shape of the garment has almost always been dictated by the pattern of the print. As a textile designer with no fashion training in dressmaking, she found it very easy to reject the traditional conventions of pattern cutting. It was a fresh approach to the construction of clothing.

"I am tired of good taste. I want to do everything wrong and get a result that is of value and valid as well."

Zandra Rhodes' imagination is suffused with *Colour*. Even in her student years at the Royal College of Art, she worked long hours to perfect original colour combinations. This is an essential part of her exploration with print, and a vital component of the finished textile before it is cut to create the final garment.

1977 saw a turning point in her career as she focused on the deconstruction of the fabric itself, although she first slashed printed silk in 1970. The Conceptual Chic collection earned her the title of the High Priestess of Punk. Although the political upheavals at the time had some influence, it was more the anarchic treatment of the fabric that shaped this next period of her work. In the section on *Technique* we take a close look at the results of these experiments with the treatment of fabric and print.

The Dress, style number "73/44", has become Rhodes' most popular design. We have selected ten of the best examples of this iconic garment. Produced every season since 1973, it is this dress that is emblematic of Zandra's belief that a good idea should not be abandoned for the sake of fashion.

If one looks closely at the textiles one is struck by the obvious influences that her world travels have had on her work. *One World* presents her cultural inspirations, such as Welsh knitting, English Medieval costumes, Chinese silks, Kenyan patterns, Australia's Ayers Rock, American cowboys, Mexican sombreros and many more.

Finally, *The Woman* is a collection of portraits chronicling her aesthetic evolution as documented by the many different photographers. Each portrait is from a different period of her creative life and will hold significance for the viewer, bringing back memories from specific times, from the 1960s to the present day.

Curating the exhibition, we drew on our years of experience working with Zandra Rhodes. To design the exhibition we chose the celebrated art director Michael Howells, to bring a new vision to the Zandra Rhodes experience.

Zandra Rhodes mastered her aesthetic through sheer perseverance and the conviction that she had something to say. Never one to deviate from her path, she remains determined to create a radical and colourful visual metaphor of her life and experience.

Gity Monsef
Creative Director
Fashion and Textile Museum

backstage
photograph by
Clive Arrowsmith,
model Nell Campell,
1977

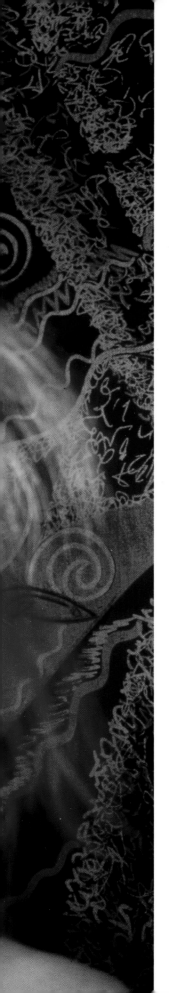

the art of textiles
by Brenda Polan

To tour an exhibition of a lifetime's work by Zandra Rhodes is to be caught up once more in the exuberant sensuality of the late 1960s when the Portobello Road supplanted Carnaby Street and Kensington as the heart of the fashion revolution. It is to live again in that moment when a passionate, questioning generation seized fashion and remade it for its own purposes.

Zandra Rhodes graduated from the Royal College of Art in 1964 at a key moment in the history of fashion. Mary Quant, Sally Tuffin and Marion Foale, Kiki Byrne, Barbara Hulanicki's Biba, Jean Muir and John Bates had pared away fashion's stale bourgeois pretensions, its middle-aged timidity. Fashion had embraced and celebrated the youthful body; now it was ready use it as a template upon which to construct flights of imaginative creativity previously equalled only in theatre and art.

By 1968 the fashion journalist, Brigid Keenan, writing in Nova magazine, was to report, 'Fashion is experiencing one of the most interesting dilemmas of its history. There is a state of anarchy.' In 1969, the American designer, Betsey Johnson, said that fashion's leaders were now 'the kids who put it all together themselves', mixing vintage clothing with ethnic dress in order both to distance themselves from any conventional middle-class fashion system and the values it represented, and to express the open-minded eclecticism, the romantic inclusiveness of their peace-and-love philosophies.

These were the clothes of dissent. And it suited the cultural commentators observing fashion for the first time to believe that each exotic outfit affected by the fashionable was a unique expression of an individual psyche. Women's Wear Daily egged them on. In 1968 it offered, 'Finding a look is almost like going through analysis... To find a personal expression of beauty, one has to search the soul.'

But it was not, of course, that simple. Or, rather, it wasn't that difficult. For most people the exuberant eclecticism was filtered and tamed through the eye and hand of one of a cadre of extraordinarily sensitive and talented designers working in Paris as well as London. What could have been ragbag chic became a djellabah by Thea Porter, a peasant dirndl by Yves Saint Laurent or by Ossie Clark in a Celia Birtwell print inspired by Leon Bakst, a cowhide bolero by Stephen Burrows, an embroidered shift by Bill Gibb, a glorious printed caftan by Zandra Rhodes.

Clothes had never been so beautiful or so exciting. And, launching her first solo collection in 1969, Zandra Rhodes was foremost among the brilliant designers of a brilliant period.

Zandra Rhodes trained as a textile designer and she is still one of the most creative and influential print designers in the world. As a fashion designer she is self-taught, driven by her habit of conceiving print and garment as one magical whole. The current exhibition is designed to demonstrate this process – just as is the book, The Art of Zandra Rhodes. 'In my original concept for the book,' she wrote, 'I was inspired by a fabulous book of water-colour drawings by Max Tilke, Costume Patterns and Designs. In this, all the garments are laid out clearly, just as butterflies are displayed in showcases.' While it is essential to see how stunning the clothes look on the body, nothing explains them better than seeing them laid flat in this way.

Zandra Rhodes is gloriously didactic. Rather like her contemporary, Vivienne Westwood, she has something of a mission to explain. 'I really want the people who come to the exhibition to go away understanding how I work,' she says. 'So we will take them through the process of design, of making a silk screen and choosing the dye colours, of cutting the garment from the printed fabric, sewing it and then adding all the signature details like the slashing, the pinking, the reversed seams.'

The designs are, of course, drawn flat – but they exist simultaneously in the designer's mind in the necessary three dimensions. 'First of all,' she says, 'having drawn the design, I think, "Do I like the pattern?" Then, I try the paper on myself and have a look at it on a big scale. I'm thinking of the print making a statement for the garment, rather than the garment just chopping into the print.'

It is that organic approach that makes Rhodes's clothes unique. Others, inspired by her, have tried to imitate her method. None have succeeded in equalling her results. No other designer has the same mastery of reference, colour, pattern, proportion and spatial impact. None has anything like the innate sense of theatre, the courage or the confidence.

She attributes the latter quality to the influence of her 'very strong' mother, Beatrice, a lecturer in fashion at the Medway College of Art. Zandra was born in Chatham, Kent. Her father was a lorry driver and she describes her background as working class. Fashion, however, was in her genes. Her mother, Beatrice, had been a fitter in the Parisian couture house of Worth before teaching fashion design. 'The strongest influence in my childhood,' she says, 'was undoubtedly my mother. She gave me my name. She actually wanted to call me Xandra – as in Alexander – but was persuaded people would not know how to pronounce it. So I became Zandra.

'She was an exotic woman, dramatically dressed, stylish and chic, always immaculately and heavily made-up, very opinionated, dominating our house, dazzling my childhood, embarrassing me in my awkward years; but ultimately being my strength and my direction.'

On leaving school Zandra enrolled at Medway College of Art but very deliberately steered clear of fashion. 'I didn't want anyone to know the connection and I took elaborate pains to avoid her.' Instead, she studied textile design with the intention of making a career in furnishing fabrics. During her first term at the Royal College of Art, however, she discovered she couldn't go on fighting her fate, gave in and switched to fashion textiles. She was, she says, much influenced by the work of Emilio Pucci and by the pop art images of Andy Warhol and Roy Lichtenstein. Her graduate collection was based on a theme of medals and was inspired by David Hockney, a fine art student two years ahead of her at the Royal.

On graduating she lived with her boyfriend, television and textile designer, Alex MacIntyre, in Notting Hill, then only in the early stages of gentrification, and launched her career as a freelance textile designer. Although she earned commissions from Tuffin and Foale, she was not an instant success. She took a teaching job at Ravensbourne where she met the fashion designer, Sylvia Ayton with whom she set up in partnership.

Together they opened the Fulham Road Clothes Shop in Fulham, which attracted considerable press attention. In the end Zandra's style proved too distinctive for any such creative partnership to endure. Her prints dominated, dictating the form of the garment; there was little room for input from anyone else. The clothes, witty, brilliantly coloured, slightly ethnic and very romantic, were stunningly beautiful and entirely her own. In 1969 she produced her first solo collection of clothes. They were bought by, among other stores, Fortnum & Mason in London and Henri Bendel in New York.

'I found out,' she says, 'from my earliest experiments in the world of textile design, that I was like no one else and fitted into nobody else's shoes. That meant that all along I was the best promoter and advertisement for my clothes. So, since I did a new look every six months, I had to change my appearance every six months. I used myself as a canvas with no compromises.'

In doing so she created what we were later to learn to call a brand. She does not underestimate its part in fixing her in the public's imagination. She is still the most widely-known name of her generation of British designers.

In fact, her experiments with cosmetics and hair dye were a profound influence on the professionals working in those fields. Many credit her with inspiring their very choice of career. Her long hair is currently a glorious fuchsia but once it was green. Green? 'Around 1970 I went to Leonard with some green hair dye and had him put some streaks in. I stayed green until about 1980; having been to China I went pink. Now my hair is grey. At one time I thought I'd go natural but I didn't feel "me".'

Fuchsia, however, does. Tiny, slender and as exotically beautiful and brilliant-hued as ever, Zandra Rhodes now divides her time between her penthouse home above the Museum of Fashion and Textile she founded in Bermondsey and her home in Southern California. Although she still travels a good deal to promote her fashion label, she lives most of the time on the Pacific ocean front in Del Mar, just outside La Jolla in California, with her partner of eighteen years, Salah Hassanein, the ex-president of Warner Brothers Theatres.

15

'If it were not for him,' she says, 'I would be here in Britain all the time. I am a British designer. I do think that, as much as people might be interested in my work, it is largely because it has a British aspect.' That's a tongue-in-cheek way, perhaps, of referring to the extent to which she is still 'referenced' by other designers. The work of her generation has recently provided a rich resource for a younger generation.

Along with Bill Gibb, Ossie Clark, Celia Birtwell, Moya Bowler, Janice Wainwright, Marion Foale and Sally Tuffin, and John Bates, she shifted the world's perception of British fashion from either classically conservative or "outrageous" to ground-breakingly creative and gloriously baroque. The approbation earned by her generation was to become the foundation of the confidence with which later generations – down to John Galliano, Alexander McQueen and Stella McCartney – went out to shape international fashion.

'Seeing my work again as we prepare it for the exhibition makes me see the validity of what I do,' muses Zandra Rhodes. 'I look at it and I think, I still believe in that. I would like to be thought to be like Charles James, who was not fully appreciated in his lifetime. The clothes are all like your children that you rediscover; they evoke memories as you press them... Some are now 30 years old and half the people who are going to see them didn't live through these adventures.

'It comes on you by accident. I get asked to do lectures all around the world. You suddenly realise that for the people you are talking to, this is history, it happened before they were born. For them it's museum fodder.'

That's not quite as dismissive as it may sound. The founder of the Fashion and Textile Museum does, after all, believe in museums and their value. 'It was always terribly important to me to preserve my work,' she says. 'I set out to keep one sample of everything I ever designed. Inevitably I have a lost a few things on the way to accident and flood. It has been like a millstone round my neck, this ever growing collection of clothing requiring vast storage facilities. At last it has a proper home.'

It gives her great pleasure, too, to exercise her rather academic interest in provenance and attribution. During her long career she has travelled far in her search for the visual and cultural stimulation that sparks her extraordinary imagination – and time-travelled too. The exhibition acknowledges her debt to India, China, Mexico, Africa, Spain and Australia, as well as ancient Egypt and Hellenic Greece, both mediaeval and renaissance Europe and the Old West. The clothes that resulted are among the most beautiful ever made anywhere - whether pastel and ethereal and utterly ingénue or in the singing pinks of India and yellows of China, ethnically bright and exotic or naughtily, darkly vampy, early tributes to the culturally subversive whether Gothic or Punk.

She is eager, too, to acknowledge the artists and designers who have influenced her work in terms of concept and rigour as well as shape and pattern. From the earliest enchantments of Sonia Delaunay, Paul Poiret and Schiaparelli to her long working friendship with the artist Andrew Logan, she is always generous in her praise. She never wavered in her admiration of Emilio Pucci – 'Even though, when I left the RCA and I was introduced to Pucci, he asked me why I didn't design in black and white?'

Another hero never flaunted feet of clay. 'I met Charles James when he was living at the Chelsea Hotel [in New York],' she remembers. 'He tried this amazing skirt on me; it was like a figure eight and you couldn't really tell whether it was trousers or a skirt. It was almost the end of his life. Halston, who supported him and got ideas from him, was a mutual friend and took me to meet him. He was always working, he never stopped, he couldn't. He went into a kind of highly focused trance.'

Although it's hard to imagine Zandra Rhodes undergoing moments of self-doubt, she confesses to wondering whether the power of the Zandra brand militates against the status of Zandra Rhodes the designer. 'Sometimes,' she says, 'I think that the fact that I have such a distinctive image and hair has detracted from my reputation for the clothes.' She reflects. And shrugs. 'The worst thing you can do,' she decides, 'is get bitter.'

This exhibition goes some way to explaining why a new generation of designers should feel their creativity fired by the colour, the baroque decorativeness, the sensuous and joyous high drama of the period. It also demonstrates why the mid eighties, with its emphasis on tailoring and power dressing, brought an inevitable eclipse for Zandra Rhodes and many of her contemporaries.

'I am rather like a blinkered horse,' she says. 'The only constant in fashion is the fact that it changes. You have to stay true to yourself through the years when fashion is inimical to your style and hope you can keep going one way or another. I could make neat little suits but store buyers did not associate me with them and did not buy them. They said the clothes did not look as Zandra Rhodes clothes should look. So I existed on my private clientele.'

There were always plenty of those, women hooked on Zandra Rhodes not because of sentimental associations with their own fading youth but because they had the confidence to stay true to their own sense of what is beautiful and unique. In the last few years, as fashion swings back towards colour and decoration, their numbers have been augmented by many younger women. 'I have had several tries at the mass market,' says Zandra, 'but what I do has to be done well and expensively. I cannot really price my work for the mass market.'

This exhibition, with its emphasis on the creative process and the labour-intensive craft techniques necessary to bring a Zandra Rhodes garment into existence, succeeds at showing exactly why not. Great artistry combined with rigorous originality and total perfectionism has never come cheap.

Above Ben Scholten and Zandra Rhodes
at the Autumn/Winter 1987
'Wish upon a star' catwalk show,
photograph by Alex von Koettlitz, 1987

side ^{by} side

by Ben Scholten
Head of design

I first became aware of Zandra's work in the early seventies through the pages of Vogue during my fashion studies at Art College in Arnhem, The Netherlands. I was completely bowled over by her prints, use of colour and unorthodox approach to shapes, choice of materials and techniques, and felt an immediate affinity with her originality.

The first time I saw her designs "live" was in 1973 at a dance event staged in one of Amsterdam's largest theatres by the cutting-edge company of Koert Stuyf and Ellen Edinoff for which Zandra had designed the costumes. I was mesmerised. The prints, the colours, the sheer volume of some of the dresses and the way they moved were stunning. I thought that this woman had to be a genius. As this was opening night I expected Zandra to be present. Although I did not know what she looked like, I spent quite some time trying to find her among the audience. To no avail, but then, what does a genius look like?

During my final year at Art College I spent three months at Zandra's studio in Porchester Road for my work experience. On graduating in 1975 I was offered a permanent position with her Company and, after a few years of working in production and dealing with anything else that needed to be done, I started to assist Zandra in designing the collections, learning how to combine the rigorous formal discipline acquired in Arnhem with the intuitive creativity that distinguishes Zandra's art.

Nowadays it is my responsibility to develop Zandra's vision independently and supervise its realisation. After Zandra has decided on the final prints I experiment with the newly printed fabric by draping it, cutting it, sometimes in despair slashing and distressing it, to arrive at a garment that emphasises and complements the print and above all enhances the female silhouette.

Our design vision is not mainstream. It is spontaneous, individual, unexpected and sometimes controversial.

For me the most memorable times with Zandra are those occasions - regrettably all too rare! - when the two of us are working side by side, away from the everyday pressures of running the company, bouncing ideas off each other. It is at times like these, that I am proud to be working with the genius that I was searching for in Amsterdam all those years ago.

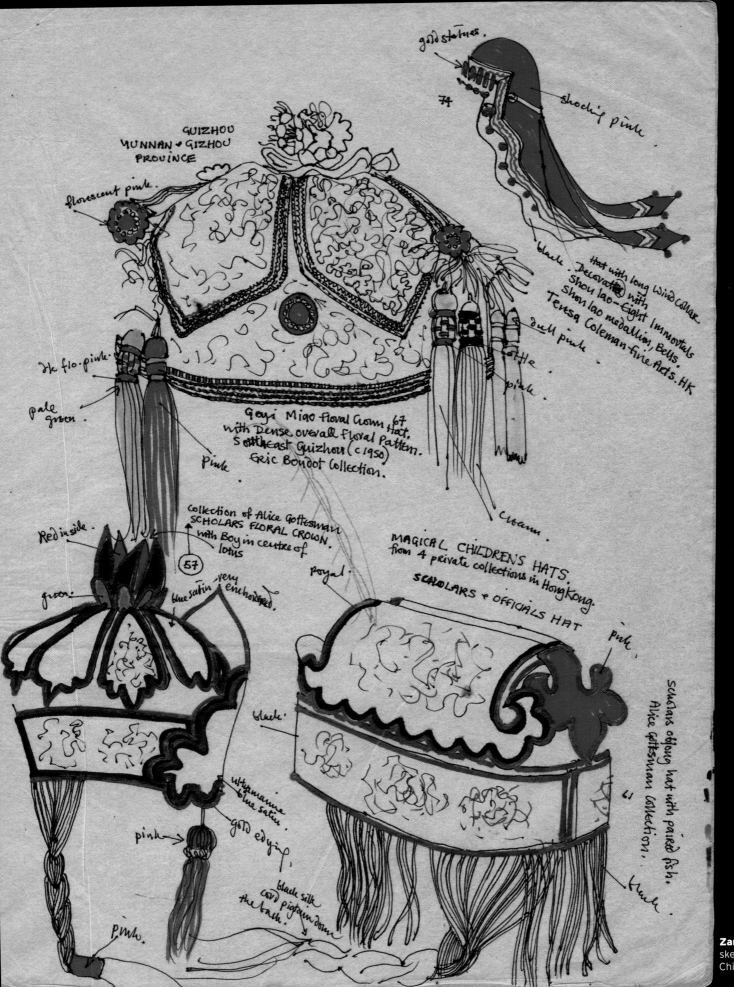

gold statues.

74

shocking pink.

black. Hat with long wind collar.
Decorated with Eight Immortals,
Shou lao — Eight Immortals, Bells.
Shou lao medallion.
Teresa Coleman Fine Arts. HK

GUIZHOU
YUNNAN & GIZHOU
PROVINCE

florescent pink.

dk.flo.pink.

pale green.

pink.

dull pink.

cattle.

pink.

Geyi Miao Floral Crown Hat,
with Dense overall floral pattern.
Southeast Guizhou (c 1950)
Eric Boudot Collection.

Cream.

Collection of Alice Gottesman
SCHOLARS FLORAL CROWN.
with Boy in centre of
lotus

57

Red inside.

green.

blue satin very
embroidered.

pink →

ultramarine
blue satin

gold edging,

black silk
cord pigtain down
the back.

P.nk.

MAGICAL CHILDREN'S HATS.
from 4 private collections in HongKong.

SCHOLARS & OFFICIALS HAT

royal.

pink.

black.

Scholars oblong hat with paired fish.
Alice gottesman collection.

black.

61

the process

In the exhibition we view an entire creative process and study an artist at work. Rhodes' final product is an art object, a testimonial to her imagination and originality.

Her designs begin with her observations of the world around her. Hers is a very personal view which begins in the pages of her ever-present sketchbook where she has drawn whatever catches her eye: knitting stitches, banana leaves, high-rise buildings catching the sun or Chinese fretwork. These inspirations will become the basis for a textile design. Even her childhood memories appear whether the zigzag, the wiggly line, the Z in Zandra or the repetition of a string of words becoming a visual dialogue for her to evolve into a pattern; suggesting a colour or inspiring a texture. These are reworked to large sheets of paper, defining and redefining the motifs and placements. It is the print that will become the dominant force in the final garment.

Vital to the next stage is the relationship of the paper design to the human body. Rhodes pins the paper design onto her own body and observes the ways in which the pattern moves with or against the form beneath it. She then begins to manipulate and reposition the textile until she achieves the desired effect. She and her textile workrooms next produce the separations, make the screens and the fabric is printed.

As a textile designer, I enjoy the discipline of the prints that have to be cut and used economically. I have to consider measurements and repeats of both the design and of the spaces in between the main design. It's both technical and artistic and it dictates the end product. I am proud to be a textile designer. It is my métier first and foremost,' she says. From the printed sample lengths the fabric is sometimes draped on a stand to create garments or sometimes laid out flat. The printed design is cut out or around so the print becomes the shape that informs the final silhouette of the garment. This is done by means of printing paper with the textile print and the pattern is drawn on the paper in heavy lines, grading included. The sheer fabric is then overlaid onto the printed paper and the printed chiffon pattern matched with the pattern below. The cutter can then cut out by seeing the lines underneath.

The Zandra Rhodes vision extends beyond the garment to the accessories, hair and make-up, which are integral to the theme for every show and an essential element. Even Zandra's own look is part of the world she creates. The final effect is a design that comes alive on the human body, an artistic expression of Zandra's unique interpretation of the world.

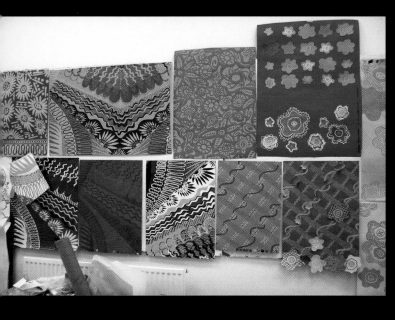

the print room

above top   repeat sticks hanging on wall, 2004

above   silk screens, 2004

right   the print table at the
                  Zandra Rhodes studio, 2004

The combination of her design and fabric prints is so unique

top left Frances Diplock, production manager, at work in the design studio, 2004

left Ben Scholten, head of design, working on a pattern, 2004

right Frances, Zandra and Ben reviewing a newly printed fabric, 2004

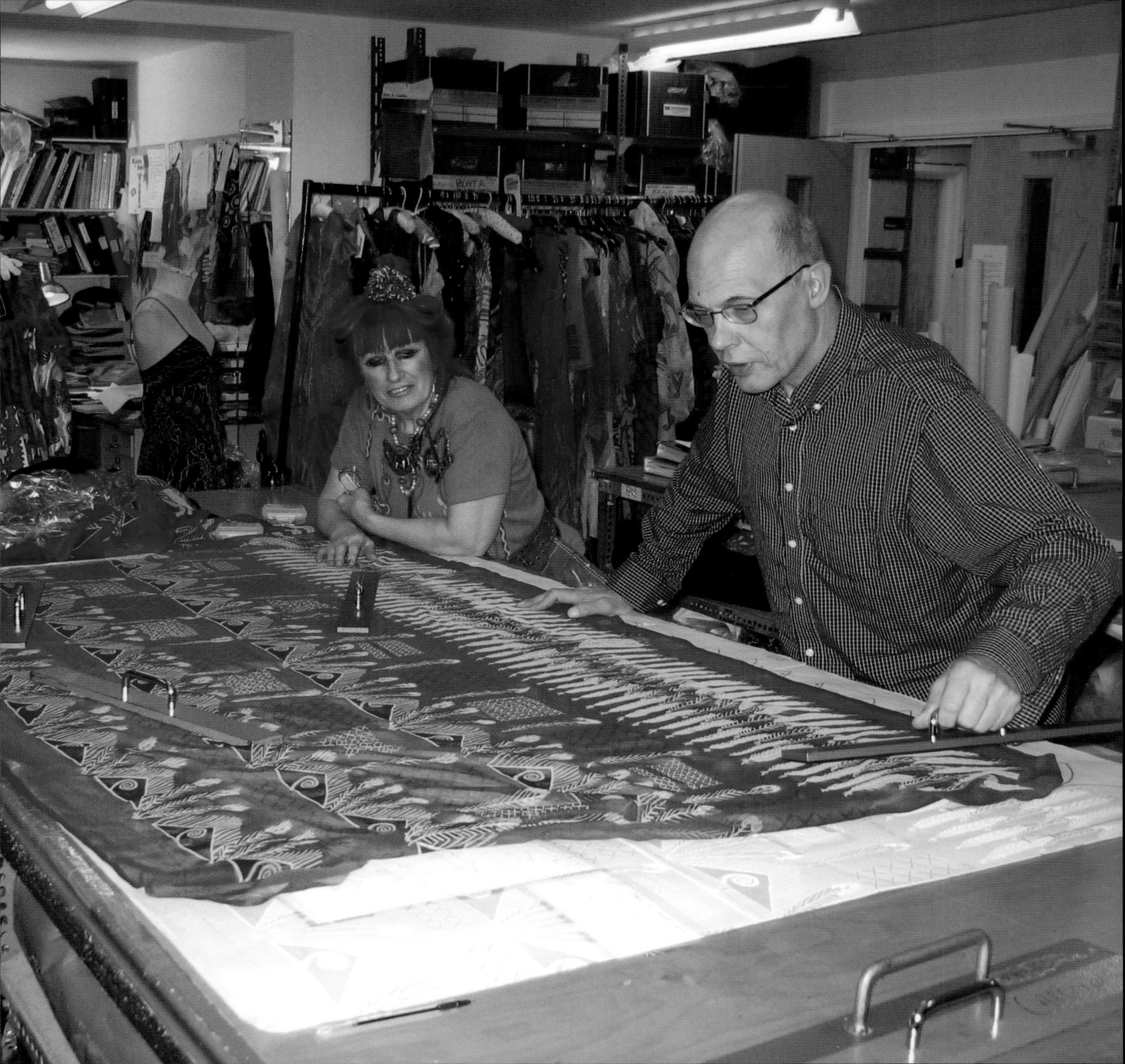

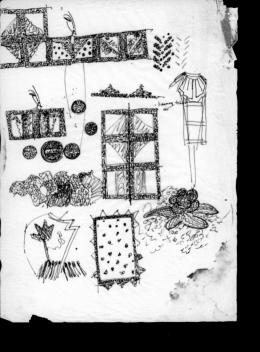

Swirling stone waves at base of large rock in pot. Summer Palace, 20 May 93. China

Exotic Rock in Pot. 15 May 93.

Over the next eight pages is shown how the process of the print of the 'Chinese Squares' developed then finally became the Chinese pagoda garment, style 79/124.

above   Zandra Rhodes' original
           sketchbook pages from
           China trip

right   The final paper artwork for
           'Chinese Squares' print, 1979

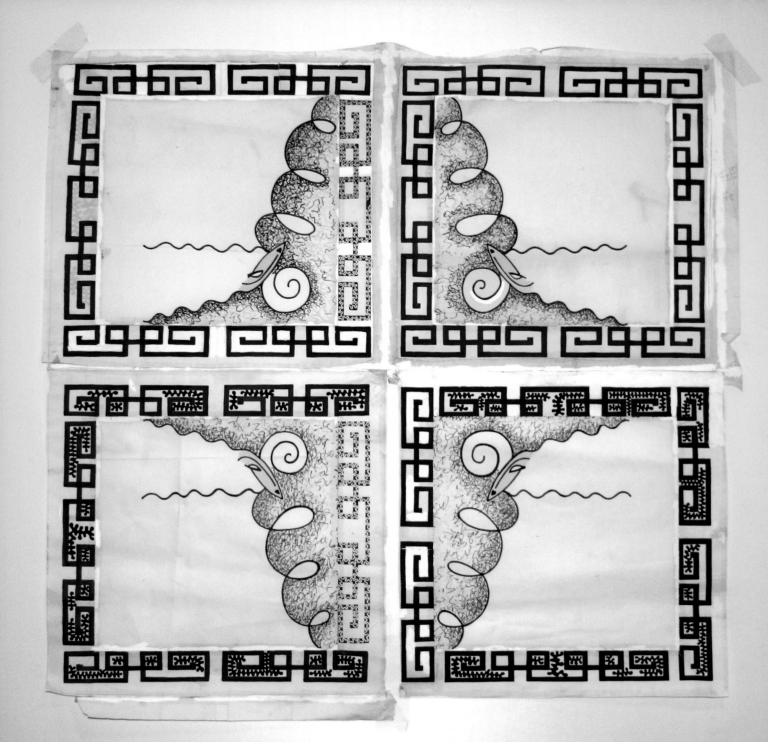

The one very special object of Zandra's, which I have always longed for, is her sketchbook.
The black hard-covered books are filled with drawings of squiggles, dots, dashes, photos, distorted
heads, big eyes, ceramic tiles, enamel pots and lots of plants and flowers. These books are the
essence of the living Zandra, the really true symbol of my friend Zandra Rhodes who is an artist.

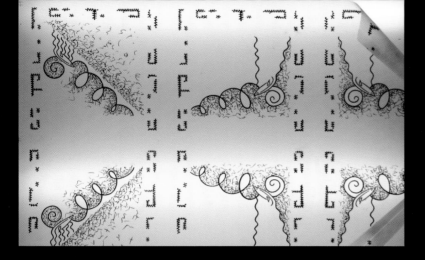

Kodatrace separations, 1979
A kodatrace is used to transfer the design on to a
silk screen, it is a positive not a negative. Screens
are developed in the following manner. The screen
is coated in a light sensive liquid. The kodatrace is
placed accurately in position on the screen, then the
screen is 'exposed' to a strong light source. All the
areas that are not exposed to the light, wash away
leaving a clear mesh through which the dye passes.
There is one kodatrace and one screen per colour.

Top kodatrace represents colour pink
Middle kodatrace represents colour white
Bottom kodatrace represents colour red
Of the original design on page 36.

right	One of the original silk screens.
There are three screens used in
total for this three colour design, 1979

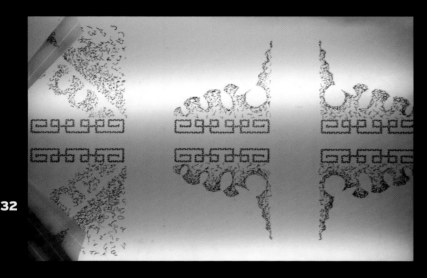

32

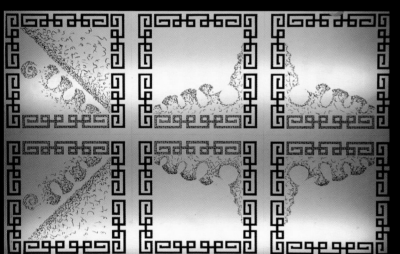

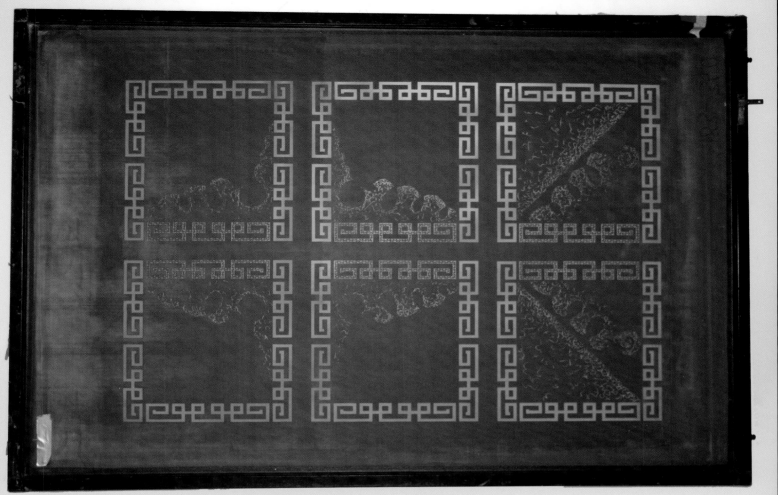

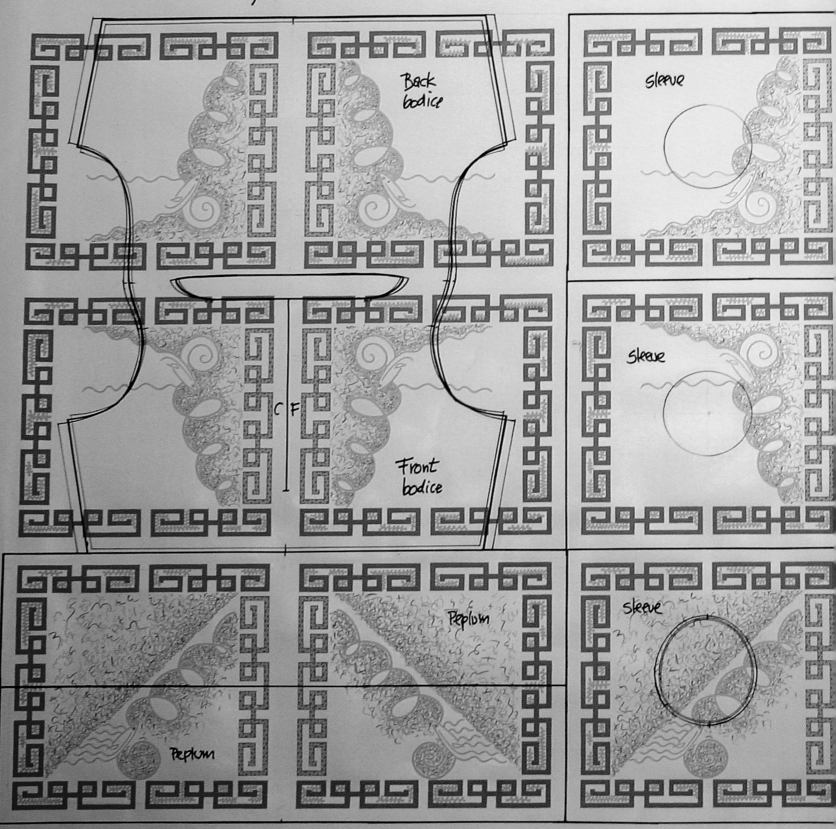

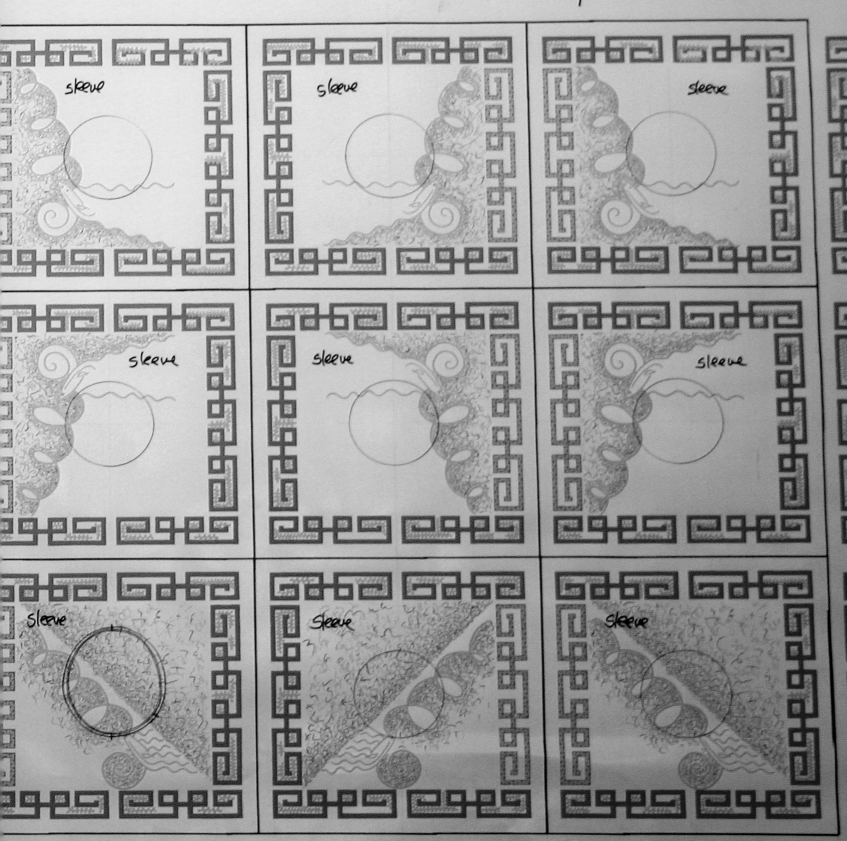

above Graded card pattern for style 79/124.
The printed fabric will be placed on top, matched to the print on the card and then cut along the lines as marked on the card.

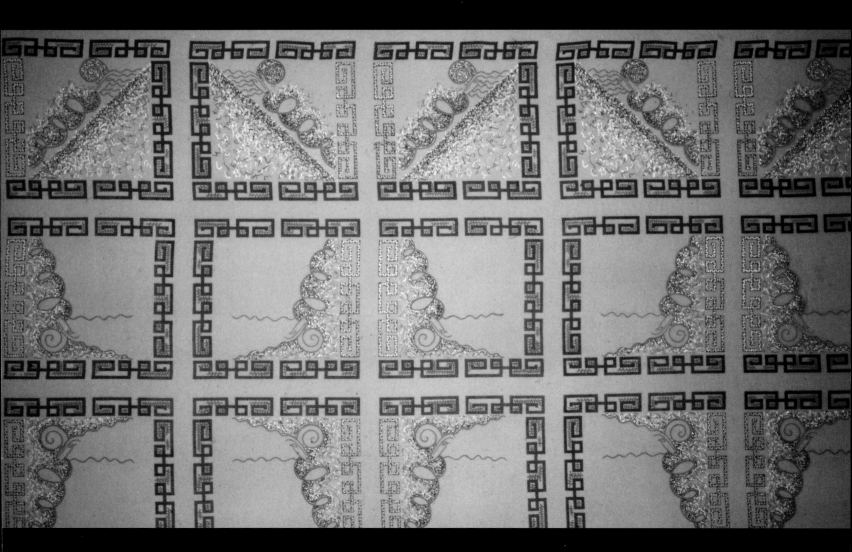

top   photograph by Conrad Santavicca

above   Length of "Chinese Squares" fabric.

right   Blouse, 1979, Style 79/124
Blouse in silk organza with pagoda sleeves in jade green, printed with "Chinese Squares" print in Chinese lacquer red, white and pink.

Skirt, 1979, Style 79/141
Skirt in silk organza with deep stitched and boned jade green waist band, printed with "Magic Heads" print.

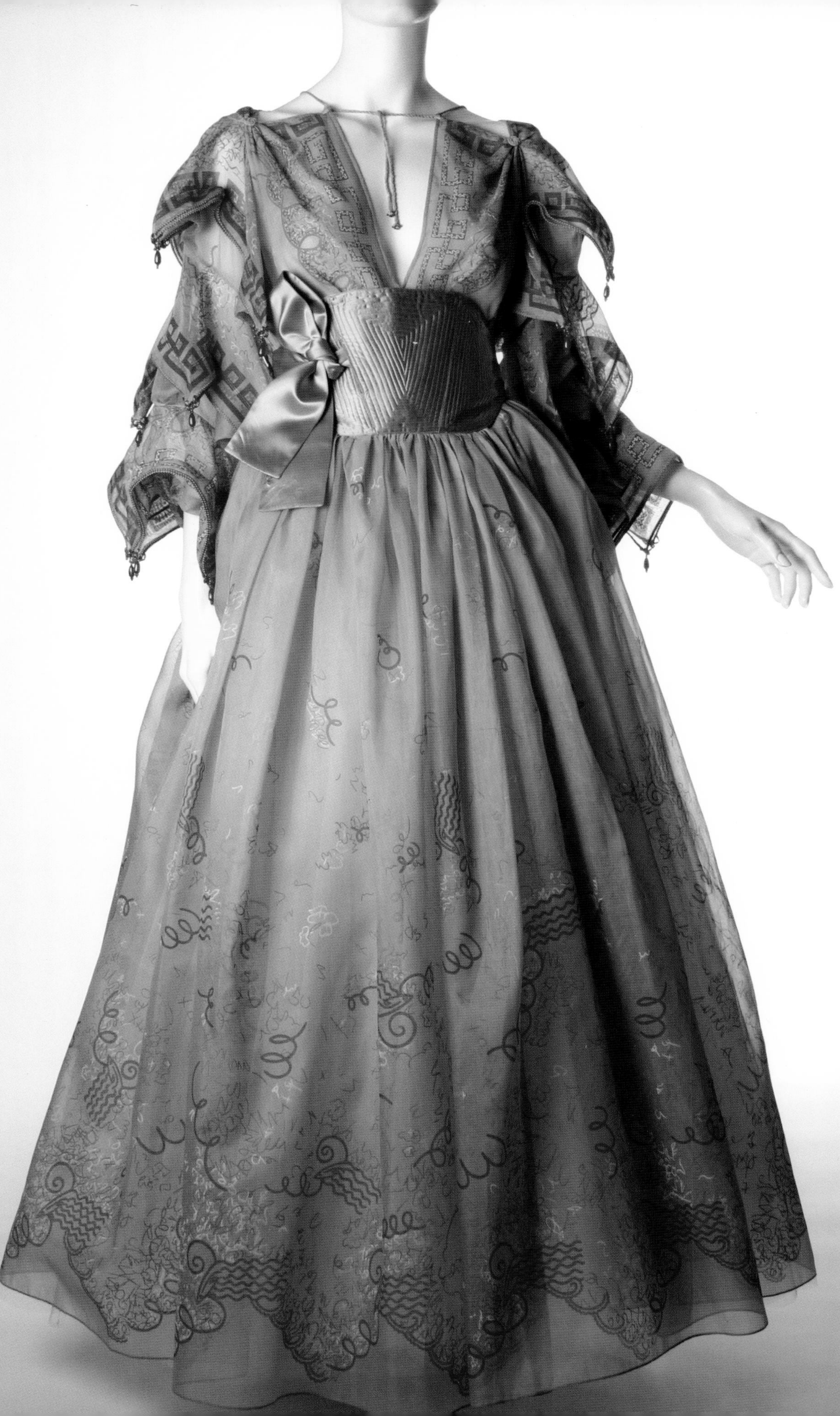

s^{the}hape

Zandra Rhodes is first and foremost a textile print designer. Several years of selling her unique and forward thinking print designs after her graduation from the Royal College of Art in 1964 had met with only mixed results. Her work with fashion designers had led her to believe that most of them were unable to recognise the potential of a print to enhance and enrich the garment. In the main, what they did was merely to cut up all the existing fabric.

Eventually Rhodes took the leap and created her first collection in 1969. Inspired by the cuts and shapes of ethnic clothing, she began the process of developing garments that followed the shape of the textile print itself. An autodidact when it came to fashion design, Rhodes' work was so original precisely because of this. She did not follow the conventions of pattern cutting and dressmaking because she had never studied these except at school so Rhodes had a totally different viewpoint when creating. This allowed for an entirely fresh approach to the construction of clothing. Other fashion designers make paper patterns that create the silhouette. With Zandra's technique the cutting of the design out of the printed textile leads to the creation of the shape. Hers is non-constructive clothing where the print is the dominating factor that dictates the design of the resulting dress.

When studying her work of this period, we begin to see the development of the Rhodes hallmark. She has allowed the motifs and inherent shapes of her print design to dictate the silhouettes of her clothing. In this way lines and circles become necklines and sleeves, repeats and edges are cut around to become shaped edges of jackets and dresses. This idea continues to be explored in the current collections of the House of Zandra Rhodes, and has been an integral part of her designs for 35 years.

left   Viva magazine photograph by Art Kane, 1974

below   Flats of "Chevron Shawl" calico coat, 1970

right   Coat, 1970, Style 70/23
Coat in "Chevron Shawl" print. The print "Chevron Shawl" is a stylised fringed shawl on unbleached calico. The edges of the fringe are cut out and stitched around to show the print on either side. The calico is bagged out and quilted. On the body the tasselled fringe drapes downwards.
(Donation of Evangeline Bruce estate)

44

Take Titania wings—
ballet of gauze
and dancing feathers

Palest azure wisp flying pendants, ending in sugar pink feathers, *opposite*. Catch it at the waist, above cream silk jodhpurs gathered from a wide ruched hipband. Canvas boots handpainted by Pablo & Delia, 15 gns exclusive of painting, to order, The Chelsea Cobbler. Their painted leather choker to order, Mr Fish. Pendant at waist, £4 15s, Hope & Eleanor, Chelsea Antique Market. Lipstick, Biba's Mahogany. Dog rose pink chiffon figured in periwinkle, *left*, fading away to a featherstorm of pink and red. Silk jodhpurs. Both dresses, by Zandra Rhodes, at Fortnum & Mason. Choker, £16, at Thea Porter. Rings, The Purple Shop, Chelsea Antique Market. Lipstick, Boots' no 7 Clover Haze. Hair, Michael of Michaeljohn. Sizes, colours, see Stockists

HENRY CLARKE

eft   Jacket, 1970, Style 70/4
Jacket and skirt in shocking pink silk chiffon printed with "Chevron Shawl" print. When on the body the tasselled feather fringe hangs downwards and moves freely like a real fringe. The print is of a stylised shawl with fringe. The points are trimmed with white feathers and all the edges are hand-rolled.
(Zandra Rhodes Archives loaned to the FTM)

above   British Vogue, photograph by Henry Clarke, 1970

She has contributed joy, freedom, exoticness, colour and several dashes of late Matisse to the world of fashion.

left   Dress, 1970, Style 70/33
Dress in black silk chiffon printed with "Indian Feather Sunspray" print in turquoise, ginger and cobalt blue. The centre seam flutes because the seams are on the outside and the scallops of the print have been cut out to form a cascade. The sleeves are made by cutting around the large feather sunsprays. All edges are hand-rolled.
(Zandra Rhodes Archives loaned to the FTM)

below   Flat of "Spiral Shell" dress, 1973

right   Dress, 1973, Style 73/7
Dress in white with "Spiral Shell" and "Reverse Lily" prints. It has been cut out along the curve of the "Reverse Lily" print for the yolk seam and around the inside curve of the shell spirals. This causes the dress to fall in narrow fishtails at the sides and the line of the "Reverse Lily" print supplies the bust detailing.
(Zandra Rhodes Archives loaned to the FTM)

Zandra was breaking all the rules, creating pieces that were wild, beautiful and ethereal. She is an original. She embraces new ideas completely and is a delight to work with, being both down-to-earth, and wonderfully creative. She encapsulates what is so exciting about British fashion, she's brave, instinctive and always true to herself.

Jane Shepherdson

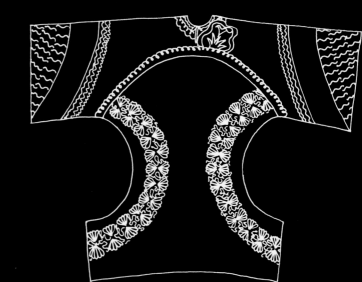

48

Zandra's clothes were, and are, completely and utterly transformative. They can turn anybody, no matter who they are, into the most exotic groovy fantasy on earth. Zandra's creations are - thank God! - the antithesis of career clothing. They are not designed to make the wearer look efficient or competent. They are designed to transform the wearer into a hallucination. A Zandra frock can take a horsey aristocrat and transform her into a gorgeous wood nymph. A Zandra frock can take a hard-boiled Hollywood agent - and make her into a bohemian glamour-puss.

Simon Doonan
Author and Creative Director
Barneys New York

previous pages   Jacket, 1971, Style 71/28
Jacket in cream and pink in "Spiral Shell" print. The jacket drapes in curves because the underarm seams follow the lines dictated by the print. The base of the jacket is gathered into the contained line of the edge quilting.
(Donation of Dasha Shenkman in the name of her mother Belle Shenkman)

below   Flats of jacket, Style 71/28

right   Dress, 1970, Style 70/35
Dress in yellow printed with "Indian Feather Sunspray".
The skirt hangs in tiny featherlike fronds because the printed feathers in the sunspray have been cut around.
The feather motif is emphasised by the giant ostrich feather hanging from the ethnic inspired velvet bodice.
All edges are hand-rolled.
(Zandra Rhodes Archives loaned to the FTM)

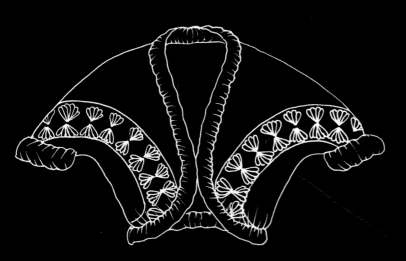

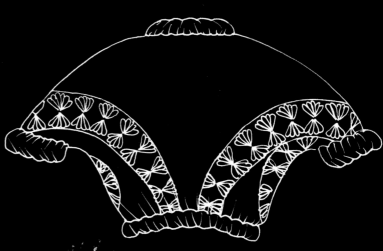

Be a latter day Infanta,
in charted gold satin...
be a frill...

54

above left Kaftan, 1970, Style 70/32
Short kaftan in white silk chiffon printed with cobalt, ginger and turquoise in "Indian Feather Sunspray". The edges of this square cut shape are cut out along the lines of the print. The centre front fabric at the bust and hem hang down in front of the garment because the edges of the feathers in the print have been cut out. All edges are hand-rolled.
(Zandra Rhodes Archives loaned to the FTM)

left Flat of kaftan, Style 70/32

right New York Times Magazine photograph by Lisa Eisner, 2002

colour

When one thinks of Zandra Rhodes, one immediately thinks also of shocking pink. In her oeuvre, we can see a thematic exploration, with similar colour schemes surfacing and resurfacing. An example of this idea of an exploration of a group of colours can be seen in her use of strong yellows mixed with red, deep blue, and violet. These combinations are a continuous theme still seen in the current Zandra Rhodes collections. The strength of her work is apparent in these combinations. Initially regarded as garish, we appreciate their vibrancy and freshness.

As important as the colour used in the prints, the colour of the fabric itself, be it chiffon or felt, is an integral part of Rhodes' designs. The unexpected combinations of fabric, print and colour challenge our response to fashion and require us, as viewer, to reconsider the very idea of "good taste".

Rhodes has also explored many subtle and harmonious colour schemes in her career, developing a sophisticated colour sense with the palest of tones. These can be seen throughout her oeuvre in pale pink, sea foam greens, delicate aqua and white. Similarly she can take the most mundane of colours, charcoal grey, and revitalise it by printing on it the unexpected.

Like all of the elements of Zandra Rhodes' work, her continued explorations of colour stories have developed, and still develop, organically. Hers is a career where no ideas are ever lost and forty years later we can still appreciate the power of those combinations.

Colour way samples of Zandra Rhodes prints, 2004

above   photograph by Norman Eales, 1970

right   Kaftan, 1970, Style 70/10
Kaftan in "Indian Feather Border" print on red silk chiffon; separate
strips of "Feather Border" hanging from ruched yoke and sleeves
gathered horizontally; trimmed with velvet ribbons.
(Zandra Rhodes Archives loaned to the FTM)

Over the past thirty-five years, whenever I need a dose of color, I know where to get an immediate high. I pick up the phone and call the fabulous Zandra or I dress up in one of my many Zandra Rhodes flamboyant creations. Whether she is designing clothes, planning museum exhibitions, or creating the ambience for opera, for ballet or for her own home, there is always an explosion of color.

Sandy Schreier

Coat, 1971, Style 71/34
Coat dress in quilted satin in "Frilly" and "Button Flower" print. The pattern is arranged in three rows in the "Frilly" print. The skirt is made from 13 complete circles. The first consisting of one circle, the second of three circles and the third of nine circles. The sleeves printed with "Button Flower" print. Plain black satin bodice with appliquéd "Button Flower" motif.
(Zandra Rhodes Archives loaned to the FTM)

Indian Sari collection,
photograph by Swapan Mukergee,
mirrored jewellery by Andrew Logan

below Dress, 1982, Style 82/61
Dress in charcoal grey silk chiffon printed with lemon, green, red and ginger
in "Jungle Trail" design. Dress with gathered waist and asymmetrical hem cut
around the line of the print. Black tulle shoulder inset, satin stitched around
the print. Satin sash. (Zandra Rhodes Archives loaned to the FTM)

right Flower Fairy's collection, photograph by Stan Ripton, model Andrea Dellal, 1982

Technique

It is important to note that in the treatment of fabric and print Zandra Rhodes has consistently moved beyond the surface and into and through the cloth itself. This forms an important element of her design as it exemplifies the experimental approach that has informed her career.

Beginning in the early seventies, Rhodes began to play with the idea of featuring external seams. Predating the deconstructionist school of design by two decades, her explorations would take interior construction and sewing detail, transforming them into decorative elements that would define the shape and structure of the garments, a visual exoskeleton to carry the design forward. These details moved from raw, pinked edges on slashed silk tunics and dresses to elaborately stitched arabesques in fluid matt jersey. Further inspiration came from the Victoria and Albert Museum, where slashed Elizabethan silks were on display. This provided not only the base for a textile design, "Sparkle", but gave Rhodes the impetus to cut into the fabric as well, hand cutting slashes into the printed silk garments.

When she began to move the focus of the collections away from printed textiles, she was picking up on the zeitgeist of the mid-seventies, when patterned, flowing, feminine dresses no longer seemed appropriate. It was at this stage that her design started to take on a harder edge as she began to experiment with "the beautiful qualities of a tear" that were to be so characteristic of the punk style. Her work at this time made a design feature of safety pins straddling slashed holes in clinging jerseys that were beautifully stitched and jeweled.

above   photograph by Bishin Jumonji, 1971

left   Coat, 1971, Style 71/19
"Dinosaur" coat in heavy natural coloured felt. Lining in "Button Flower" print on satin, with appliquéd "Button Flower" motifs at shoulder; wide zigzag cut edges as decorative outside seam detailing.
(Zandra Rhodes Archives loaned to the FTM)

SCISSORED

Pagoda shift of cream silk
printed with scissored red,
turquoise and blue,
silhouette clipped with pinking shears.
Centre laced open sleeves,
is smothered back
to the longer dress beneath
printed at the hem and set the long
whisking sleeves finished
with small silk buttons.
Both dresses slashed through
with tiny slits at centre too.
Big padded blue heart, little silver
padded hearts tied into the ends
of the plaited hair.
Heavy white tights, Mary Quant.
Ivory suede wedges, Kurt Geiger.
Hair by Oliver at Leonard.

SILKS

Blouse over dress over knickerbockers,
three wisps of cream silk
with print of red, turquoise, blue.
Blouse with brilliant panne velvet back,
front and back, ostrich feathers
of violet, turquoise and electric blue,
and cascading sleeves, full, pinked,
open from elbows. Then pagoda shift
slashed and pinked round,
and slashed knickerbockers falling
in a scalloped frill. Silver padded heart
and feathers in the hair, small blue
padded hearts tied to shoes.
White shoes, Anello & Davide.
Clothes, both pages, by Zandra Rhodes
at Fortnum & Mason and Harrods.
Accessories by Pablo & Delia, at
Boston-151: The Shop at Vidal Sassoon.
GUY BOURDIN

74

SCISSORED

Zandra Rhodes' dresses are the airiest
lightly printed silks, got at by a pair
of mad enchanted scissors.
Blouses, shifts, knickerbockers
are pinked at the edges and seams,
castellated, slashed into waves of length,
cut in slits and Vs, so that every piece
streams in tiers of points and curves.
Flying with them the Soft Accessories
of Pablo & Delia,
featherweight padded hearts
in pale blue and silver leather
are hung on fine threads of leather
and mixed with pale painted sweets and wisps
of brilliant dyed feathers

SILKS

Silk dress, both pages, slashed through the print of red, turquoise, navy on cream, hem veering into ankle-length streamers cut with pinking shears at the ends, shoulder and sleeve seams sheared too. At Fortnum & Mason and Harrods. Soft padded leather collar with strings of padded pink flowers and leaves, blue padded hearts tied to the shoes, by Pablo & Delia, at Botton-151; The Shop at Vidal Sassoon. Tights, Mary Quant. White shoes, Anello & Davide. Hair by Oliver at Leonard

previous page & left   British Vogue, photographs by Guy Bourdin, 1977

right   Dress, 1971, Style 71/2
Overdress of cream silk combining
"Sparkle" and "Indian Feather
Border" prints. Silk is slashed
leaving raw cut edges.
Hem bound with silk rouleaux.
(Zandra Rhodes Archives
loaned to the FTM)

Zandra Rhodes understands that textile is a canvas not unlike a painting and effortlessly has blended her talent as a print designer with the mastery of a tailor to create a signature style that is immediately identifiable.

Cameron Silver

left top Dress, 1971, Style 71/3
Dress in "Sparkle" print white on black silk with slashes and raw cut edges; bodice hand smocked at centre front and back.
(Zandra Rhodes Archives loaned to the FTM)

left British Vogue, photograph by Clive Arrowsmith, 1971

right Top, 1974, Style 74/47
Top in black jersey with smocked front and back, pleated jersey collar and contrast 'lettuce' edges'
(Kindly loaned by Frances Diplock)

below and right   Dress, 1977, Style 77/15
Punk wedding dress. The long white satin sash with white
jersey panel is attached with beaded safety pins and chains
and tied as a halter. Black stitched contrast edges.
Underdress with high side split, long train decorated with
holes, beaded safety pins and chains.
(Zandra Rhodes Archives loaned to the FTM)

80

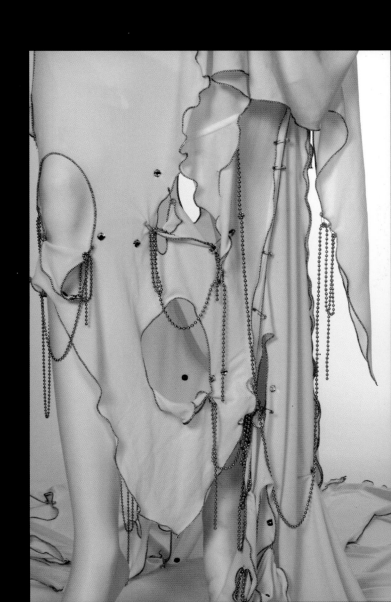

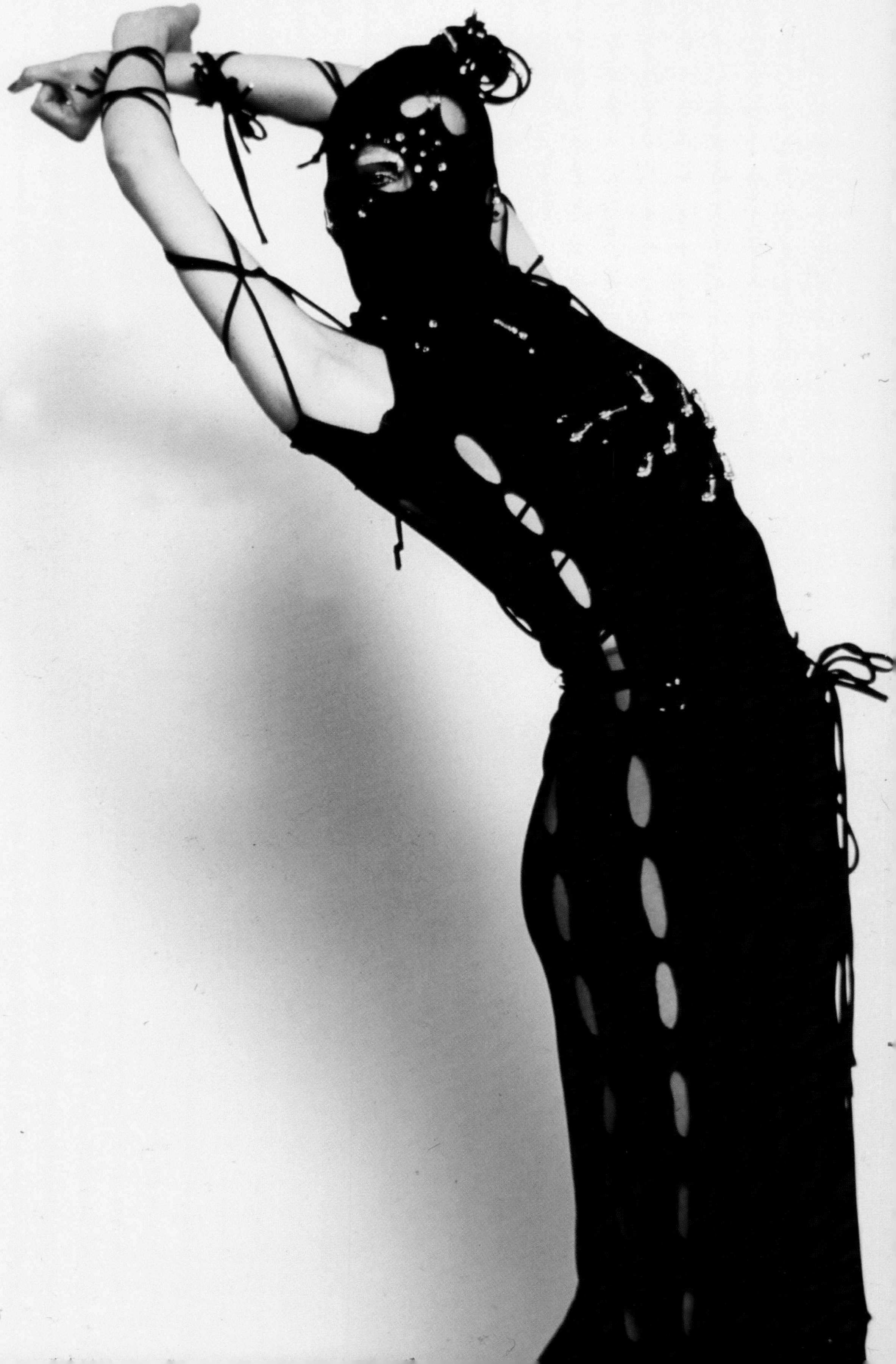

Backstage at Zandra Rhodes catwalk show,
photograph by Clive Arrowsmith,
model Nell Campell, 1977

above left

Dress, 1978, Style 78/106
Dress with tiny black satin bodice with one breast revealed.
Jersey skirt caught onto bodice with beaded safety pins.
(Zandra Rhodes Archives loaned to the FTM)

above

Dress, 1978, Style 78/31
Dress in black jersey with holes at shoulders, decorated
with chains and beaded safety pins and contrast 'lettuce'
edges, decorative holes at centre front neck.

Sash, 1977, Style 77/15
Long red satin sash with pink asymmetric jersey strip
attached with beaded safety pins, decorated with chains
and Swarovski rhinestones and contrast 'lettuce' edges.
(Zandra Rhodes Archives loaned to the FTM)

above right

Top, 1977, Style 77/18
Jersey top in black (made from four circles; one for yoke,
one for body, two for sleeves) with asymmetric holes,

above
Jacket, 1978, Style 78/65
Ultrasuede jacket with asymmetric
embroidered seams on the outside,
appliquéd "Magic Head" motif in
contrast colours; beaded with
Swarovski crystals.
(Kindly loaned by Robyn Beeche)

left and right
Backstage at Zandra Rhodes
catwalk show,
photograph by Clive Arrowsmith,
1977

Zandra Rhodes is the most exuberant, generous and colourful fashion designer who has delighted people around the world with her work. Her fashion designs are timeless and her teaching will influence designers for generations to come. Zandra Rhodes is a most important and original artist.

Mary Quant

opposite page   British Vogue,
photograph by Clive Arrowsmith,
model Pat Cleveland,

right   Dress, 1972, Style 72/11
Jersey dress in yellow with contrast
'lettuce' seam edging. Bodice insert
in"Field of Lilies" print on silk chiffon,
with contrast satin lining held in place
with satin-stitched "Lilies"; all seams
are on the outside.
(Zandra Rhodes Archives loaned to the FTM)

below right   Dress, 1971, Style 71/20
Dress in black jersey with 'lettuce'
edging, quilted satin collar and appliquéd
"Button Flower" motifs.
(Zandra Rhodes Archives loaned to the FTM)

next page   Backstage at Zandra Rhodes catwalk show
photograph by Clive Arrowsmith
from left to right
make-up by Regis
model Tina Chow
hair by Leonard of London

If you could look up Zandra Rhodes in the 20th Century Dictionary of the English Language, the definition might read:

Clothing designer and textile artist, British. First collection, 1967. First public collection, 1969. First to write on fabric. First to trace her travels from original sketchbook drawings into fabric, Zandra-izing everything from the Great Wall of China and Ayers Rock in the Australian Outback to the neon cowboy on the Las Vegas strip. First to recognize the punks as part of a fashion movement (1977). First to de-criminalize crinolines. First to bring pretty back as part of the fashion vocabulary. And first to admit that she'd like "to become one of those old women who grow old glamorously... to be larger than life."

Marylou Luther,
Editor-in-chief,
International Fashion Syndicate

the dress

In 1973, Zandra Rhodes produced what would become her best-selling garment, known to this day by its style number, "73/44". Utilizing the signature Rhodes prints, this dress would be re-introduced and re-evaluated each season and is still referenced by the house of Zandra Rhodes today.

The "73/44" is a feminine and flattering dress that has graced celebrities, royalty, models and women around the world. Working with the shape of the print, this garment has a deep V-neckline and graceful sleeves gather into a full skirt. A satin sash in a contrasting or complementary colour, another Rhodes trademark, finishes the look. It is a dress that moves and flows with the body, its prints and colour highlighting the romantic moods of Zandra Rhodes' work from that time.

This dress would come to personify an era. It was seen at dinners, parties and nightclubs and mixed the hedonism of the times, in its sheer and sexy use of chiffon, and the inherent romanticism of Rhodes' style. It was introduced in the Lovely Lilies collection, including a show stopping version in the "Field of Lilies" print and adorned with swags of silk tulle and topping a full crinoline to dramatic effect. Key textile designs of the Rhodes oeuvre would become variations of the "73/44", each adding to the allure of this one famous Zandra Rhodes style.

The best of Rhodes' work is represented by the collection of these dresses, with all the elements of her innovative designs on display. Seen in a group, with its subtle shapes and delicate colouring, the Dress is a testimony to one designer's belief in the power of feminine beauty.

previous page   Town and Country magazine,
photograph by Norman Parkinson, 1984

above   Dress, 1973, Style 73/44
Dress in dusty rose chiffon with butterfly wings. Colour
created specially for Lauren Bacall. Bodice of "Reverse
Lily" print, skirt "Field of Lilies" print. Tied with dusty rose
rose satin sash.
(Zandra Rhodes Archives loaned to the FTM)

right   British Vogue,
photograph by David Bailey,
model Anjelica Huston, 1973

I was unprepared for my first impr   of Zandra
a vivid whirl of energy, colour and   to bird
of paradise. I think she was the fi
magenta hair – she dressed in laye
she laughed and smiled a lot and w
– which struck me as unusual, since many designers of that
time took themselves extremely seriously, which involved being
unnecessarily stern with the girls.

above

right

left Dress, 1978, Style 78/3
Dress in white chiffon with gathered waist: bodice in "Mexican Fan"
print, skirt in "Mexican Sombrero" print. The fluting above the waist
accented with pleated ribbon. This colourway was specially developed
for Her Majesty Queen Elizabeth's Silver Jubilee.
(Zandra Rhodes Archives loaned to the FTM)

above Independent on Sunday, photograph by Jim Lee, 2002

**Zandra's hand-printed chiffon creations of the early seventies
brought a sense of flawless ethereal beauty to an era that was
mostly saying short, youthful, hard-edged and sexy.
In Zandra's clothes the princess emerged, and not a princess of
nasty layer cake, but a rendering of true refinement and grace.**

**She helps us see life through her rose-tinted glasses and moves
us with her visions of life with colour. If grey is for paupers,
then Zandra should be a millionaire.**

New York Times Magazine, photograph by Lisa Eisner & Roman Alonzon, 2002

this page
Dress, 1977, Style 77/9
Dress in "Mexican Dinner Plate" print on white silk chiffon in rainbow colours. Sleeves and beaded collar cut to shape of print, with hand-rolled edges and contrast satin sash. Swarovski rhinestone strip around collar edge.
(Zandra Rhodes Archives loaned to the FTM)

this Interview magazine,
page photographs by Francesco Scavullo, 1973

right Crinoline, 1973, Style 73/19
Crinoline with "V" neck. Both bodice and skirt in
"Reverse Lily" print on ivory silk chiffon; silk net
frills on skirt and sleeves following the shape of
the print.
(Zandra Rhodes Archives loaned to the FTM)

left
Dress, 1974, Style 74/47
Dress in "Lace Mountain" print on
off-white silk chiffon with "V" neck
and pleated skirt, frilled above waist by
edging skirt with pleated satin ribbon
and catching this up with silk flowers.
(Zandra Rhodes Archives loaned to the
FTM)

right
Elizabeth Jagger in German Vogue,
photograph by Alix Malka, 2002

ELIZABETH JAGGER

Die 60er und 70er wären meine Zeit gewesen.
Die Schnitte waren viel schöner als heute. Und
die Farben! Doch von Mum [Jerry Hall] konnte
ich nichts übernehmen. Sie gibt immer alles
weg. Ich mag die Läden in der Portobello Road
oder Downtown Manhattan. Und ich habe ein
paar Stones-Bühnen-Outfits. Die ziehe ich
nicht an – zu wertvoll oder too much. Als ich 13,
14 war, passten mir die Jeans von Mick: Er war
einfach sehr, sehr dünn. Als Kind habe ich vie-
le texanische Teile von meiner Cousine be-
kommen. Echt Cowgirl. Meine Kette hier ist
auch aus Texas. Der Zahn von einem Grizzly,
den mein Onkel geschossen hat. Mein Lieb-
lings-Vintage-Stück ist noch gar nicht so alt:
Mokassinstiefel, die ich vor vier Jahren von
Indianern gekauft habe. Die fallen leider all-
mählich auseinander. In echte Vintage-Schuhe
passe ich kaum rein, ich habe Schuhgröße 40.

106

left

right

Dress, 1974, Style 74/50V
Dress in van Dyck brown with deep
"V" neck, with pleated chiffon
collar and batwing sleeves.
Dress in "Lace Mountain" print.
Brown satin sash.
(Kindly loaned by Michaela Lawrence)

photographer Joe Gaffney

one world

From her first designs Zandra Rhodes has displayed an interest in the costume and construction of cultures around the world. In Rhodes' earliest solo work, the shape of ethnic costume in Max Tilke's reference work informed the dresses she would go on to produce.

As Rhodes' began to travel, her work began to absorb and reflect the broadening focus of the designer's experience. Sketching, painting and photographing everything around her, Rhodes would gather as much information as possible on her journeys, producing detailed documentation that would become the basis for successive collections.

In the studio Zandra Rhodes' would begin the design process: filtering, disseminating and reworking the fruit of her travels. As the textiles and then garments were developed, other elements of the Rhodes' style would also come to be influenced by the same eclectic aesthetic. Accessories, make-up, furnishings and music would come together to create the image of the season, to be presented in the twice-yearly fashion shows.

Some of the most memorable creations of the House of Zandra Rhodes were a result of these multi-cultural explorations. Notable among these are the Chinese Collection featuring pagoda sleeves, Rhodes' print interpretations of water circles, Chinese fretwork with traditional colourways, and accessories such as finger guards and face masks. "Spanish Impressions" was a journey through the customs and imagery of the Iberian Peninsula and culminating in a spectacular show in the inimitable Rhodes style with fantasy eye patch makeup by Phyllis Cohen, printed peacock feather tights complete with authentic castanette concerto.

In 1987, Zandra Rhodes was invited to design and produce a range of traditional saris and salwar kameez by the Indian Government, for sale and distribution in India. Rhodes' was the first western designer to produce designer clothing in the Indian style and the resulting shows in Bombay and Delhi would revolutionize the garment industry there. Rhodes was inspired by the artisans and craftspeople of India, and would feature many of their work in her own collections. A sense of English style was introduced in the fashion show as Rhodes used walking sticks, top hats and panniers on native styles.

Ancient cultures inspired Rhodes to create modern worlds out of lost civilizations. The "Mount Olympus" collection of 1983, a paean in silk noil, jersey and chiffon combined printed and slashed suede, to the Goddesses of Ancient Greece; and a journey through the splendors of the Pharaohs in the "Secrets of the Nile" replete with mummy dresses and lapis beading. It is in these collections that we can see the academic approach of research and reference that have characterized the designs of the House of Zandra Rhodes.

Also inherent in the work of Zandra Rhodes is an underlying element of Englishness. Very much a product of England, she has continually referenced the cultural identity of her home. From Cicely Mary Barker's Flower Fairies through a pastoral medievalism and the golden glories of Elizabeth I, Rhodes has continuously absorbed and redefined the national spirit in her work, a body of work that could not have been produced without it.

109

left British Vogue, photograph Barry Lategan, 1974

next page British Vogue, photograph by David Bailey model Marie Helvin, 1976

Scene III

West Coast cactus print dress, silk chiffon with bronze sequins and satin sash. 24 ct gold plated arrow earclips, Mick Milligan for Zandra Rhodes, £24. Both at Zandra Rhodes, 14a Grafton St, W.1. High-heeled slippers, Manolo Blahnik, £32, at Zapata. Tights by Bic. Hair all pages, by John at Leonard. Man's shoes, from Gamba

DAVID BAILEY

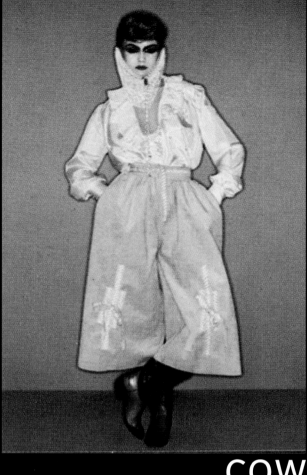

this page
photographs by Barry Lategan

far right
Top, 1975, Style U101
Top in bright turquoise ultra suede, outlined with a printed ombre border.

Trousers, 1975, Style U110
"Chap" type trousers with ombre printed ties.
(Zandra Rhodes Archives loaned to the FTM)

cowboy

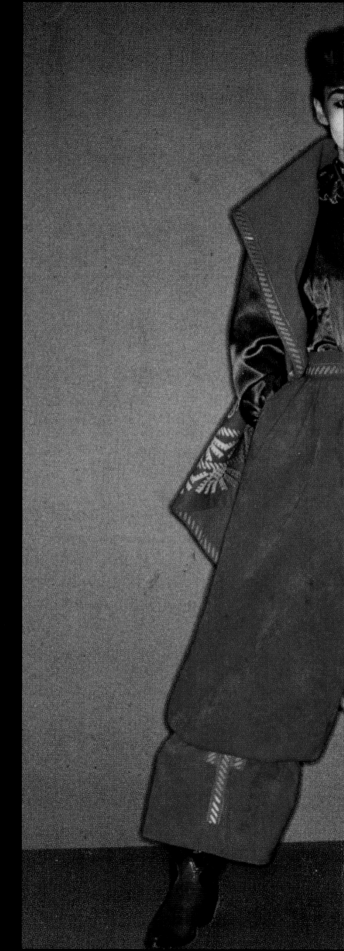

above   backstage at catwalk show,
photograph by Robyn Beeche, 1985

left   Dress, 1985, Style 85/96
Hand beaded dress in shocking pink silk
georgette with dropped waist, deep cowl back
uneven hem and sleeve edges. Beaded in
sequins and bugle beads with a Manhattan
landscape design of the Empire State
Building and Chrysler Building.
(Kindly loaned by Martha Gafford)

egypt

right   Dress, 1987, Style 87/124
Hand beaded evening dress in black silk georgette with high neck
and exposed shoulders. The beading suggests an Egyptian mummy
wrapping. Beading and stitching accented with Swarovski crystals
and dyed pearls.
(Zandra Rhodes Archives loaned to the FTM)

Spring/Summer 1987
'Secrets of the Nile' collection

hair by Trevor Sorbie
make-up by Phylis Cohen

117

hats by Zandra Rhodes Studio
jewellery by Andrew Logan
photographs by Robyn Beeche

right   Tunic, 1987, Style 87/128
Hand beaded tunic in lapis blue. Beading is done
in an interpretation of the historic winged design.
(Zandra Rhodes Archives loaned to the FTM)

Spring/Summer 1987
'Secrets of the Nile' collection

hair by Trevor Sorbie
make-up by Phylis Cohen

119

hats by Zandra Rhodes Studio
jewellery by Andrew Logan
photographs by Robyn Beeche

australia

left
photograph by Joe Gaffney

right
Dress, 1974, Style 74/5c
One-shoulder dress in "Ayers Rock"
print on red silk chiffon, over jersey
lining, quilted satin band and slashed
hand-rolled edges.
(Kindly loaned by Marjorie Rubin)

122

Spring/Summer 1983
'Mount Olympus' collection

hair by Leonard of London
make-up by Yvonne Gold
men's suit by Anthony Price

hats by Stephen Jones & Zandra Rhodes Studio
jewellery by Andrew Logan
photographs by Robyn Beeche

greece

123

mexico

Spring/Summer 1985
'India revisited' collection

hair by Leonard of London
hats by Graham Smith, Stephen Jones & Zandra Rhodes Studio
jewellery by Mick Milligan, Mark Kirkley & Zandra Rhodes Studio

make-up by Yvonne Gold
mirrored jewellery by Andrew Logan
photographs by Robyn Beeche

Spring/Summer 1982
'India' collection

hair by Leonard of London
hats by Graham Smith, Stephen Jones & Zandra Rhodes Studio
jewellery by Mick Milligan, Mark Kirkley & Zandra Rhodes Studio

make-up by Yvonne Gold
mirrored jewellery by Andrew Logan
photographs by Robyn Beeche

india

ght Tunic, 1985, Style 85/102
Long tunic in deep emerald green silk chiffon with matching narrow
trousers. Tunic printed with "Maharaja's Peacock Feathers" print,
additionally encrusted with Swarovski crystals. Swarovski rhinestone
strip at edges of collar and trousers.
(Kindly loaned by Marjorie Rubin)

africa

above **Autumn/Winter** 1981
'Africa' collection
hair by Leonard of London
make-up by Richard Sharah
african jewellery by Mark Kirkley
photographs by Robyn Beeche

right Kaftan, 1981, Style 81/79
Kaftan jacket in "Zebra Skin" print on earth
coloured silk chiffon, cut to shape of print;
edges hand-rolled and trimmed with feathers.

Dress, 1981, Style 81/87
Jersey dress with twisted shoulder straps decorated
with string, scorched wooden beads and contrast
lettuce edging.
(Kindly loaned by Joan Agajanian Quinn)

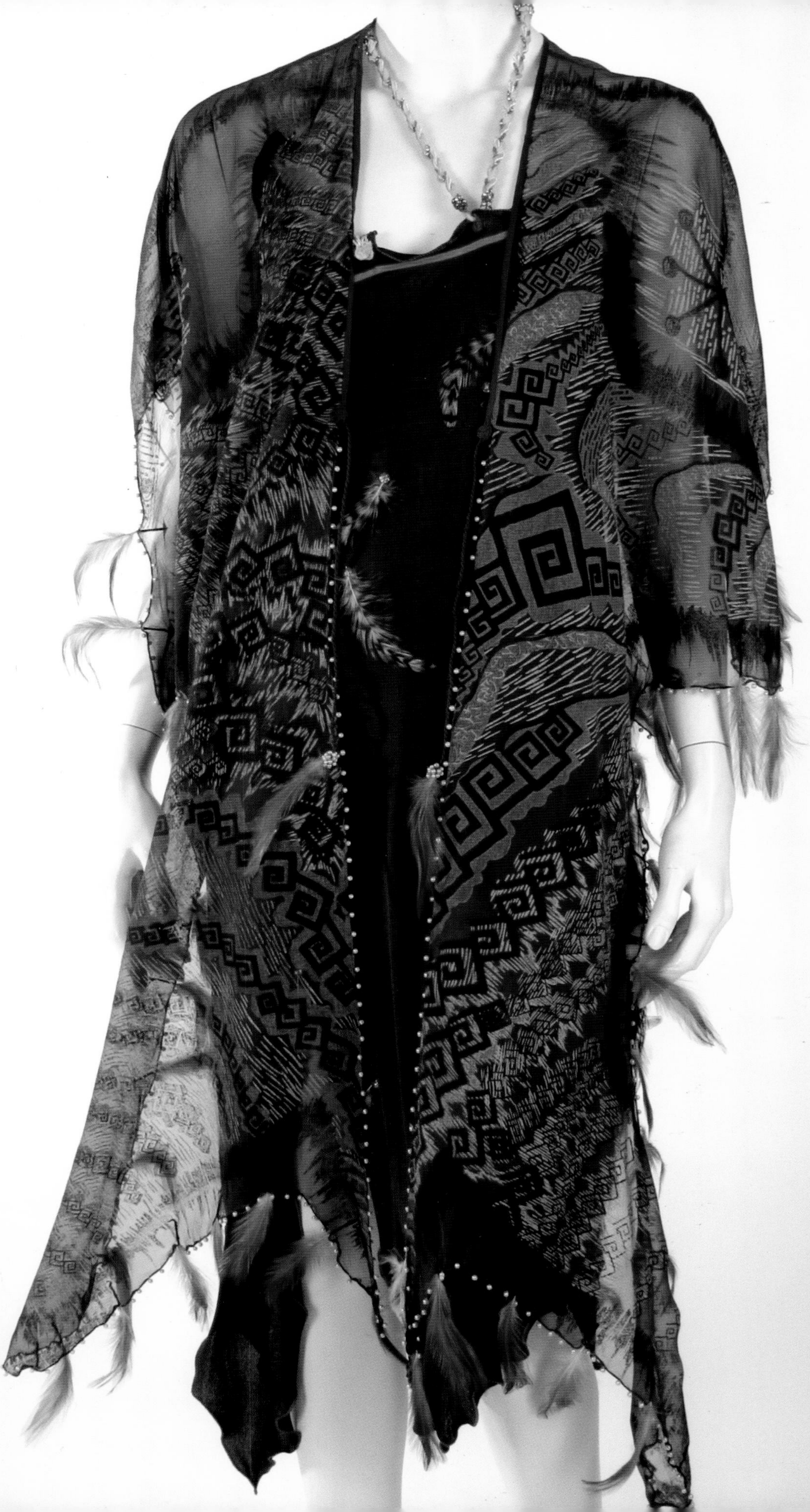

spain

Opposite page
Dress, 1986, Style 86/10
Dress in black silk chiffon printed in white with "Peacock
Feather Frills" print. Curtain ruched skirt with Swarovski
rhinestone trim and beaded fringe at hem. Pointed satin
stitched neck. (Zandra Rhodes Archives loaned to the FTM)

Spring/Summer 1986
'Spain' collection
hair by Trevor Sorbie
make-up by Phylis Cohen
hats by Stephen Jones & Zandra Rhodes Studio
jewellery by Andrew Logan
photographs by Robyn Beeche

134

Ensemble, 1981, Corset Style 81/130
Ensemble in gold pleated lamé.
Skirt held out with boned pannier.
Total outfit consists of: circular pleated
gold lamé skirt, black satin laced corset
with gold pleated sleeves, gold sash with
circular pleated swirls either side to
emphasise the pannier effect.
Inspired by the idea of the Royal Wedding
of Diana, Princess of Wales.
(Zandra Rhodes Archives loaned to the FTM)

Diana Ross, photograph by Richard Avedon

the

woman

What really struck me was her conviction to project herself and her work with equal intensity. I was also fascinated by her technique, making printed chiffon, all done by herself, which I was fortunate enough to have seen in action.

Manolo Blahnik

At what point does a creator become the creation? The image that Zandra Rhodes presents is more than a simple matter of a designer wearing the clothes she creates.

Rhodes has always viewed herself as a canvas to be experimented upon. In an even more daring way the impact of her own highly coloured and exotic appearance has in some ways exceeded that of her fashion collections and catwalk shows. A natural beauty, Rhodes has redefined her face and body as a distinctive style element.

Rhodes has been the subject of countless portraits, paintings, drawings, sculptures and photographs. It is a timeline of ideas and

I remember ZR on the London scene with her kabuki makeup and flaming magenta hair as I arrived from California. That was the mid-sixties when other exotics like David Bowie and Bill Gibb where emerging to add their magic to our lives. I never actually got to one of Zandra's fashion shows but used to peek into her shop and delight at her interviews in the media. Her total belief in herself gave us all courage.

Kaffe Fassett

139

photograph by Robyn Beeche

**Arguably, she is the best
representative of a whole era...
the most lasting contribution of
the hippie London scene,
her name,
her eyebrow,
a squiggly pattern...
can conjure the whole scene
in one's memory.**

Fredericka Hunter

She has always personified British Fashion at it's most
creative. No one used colour combinations or patterns
the ways she did. Her clothes made you an instant star.
I have had the good fortune of owning many Zandra Rhodes
designs over the years and I remember one particular dress
that I bought for the premier of The Magic Christian in
the late '60s/early '70s, which I wore to a party in 1987.
The extraordinary thing is that the dress had not dated
one bit! That is the talent of Zandra Rhodes.

Britt Ekland

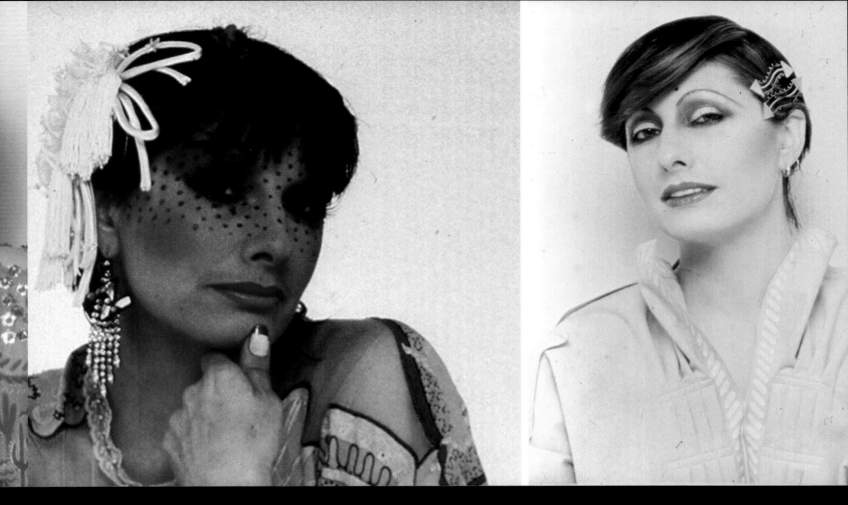

Zandra Rhodes took chiffon to the most
innovative and exotic dimension with her unique,
ethnic-inspired designs! She interpreted the
kaftan as a graphic shredded chiffon masterpiece.
No one had shredded fabric like this before –
Zandra re-thought construction – she invented
over-locked chiffon and stretched silk jersey
with the seams on the outside as frills.
These were both quintessential '70s style
statements and she created them.

Jenny Kee

Zandra kindly invited me up to "her studio".
It was like entering a dream state.
I had loved fashion for as long as I can remember,
but never had I seen anything quite like this...
her imagination is, just extraordinary,
her sense of color and design, unbeatable.
She is a true artist, in every sense.

Maxine Smith

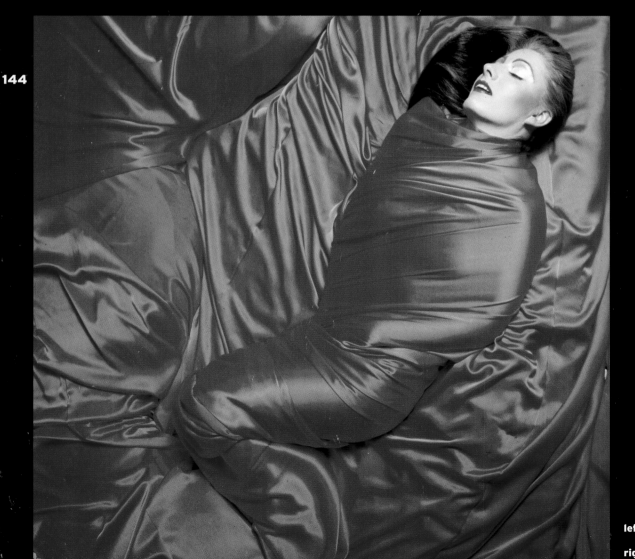

I first met Zandra when she was a very demure mousy-brown-haired student in London in the sixties. Then, out of the blue, she blossomed into a great character of enormous talent with Schiaparelli "Shocking Pink" hair with rainbow tips.

April Ashley

left photographs by Robyn Beeche

right Observer magazine
photograph by Eric Bowman, 1977

146

Zandra has been a true inspiration to me, professionally and personally.
She was one of the first people to encourage me to spread my wings and explore the opportunities in design and retail.
She is such an exotic and charismatic person.
She radiates positive energy.

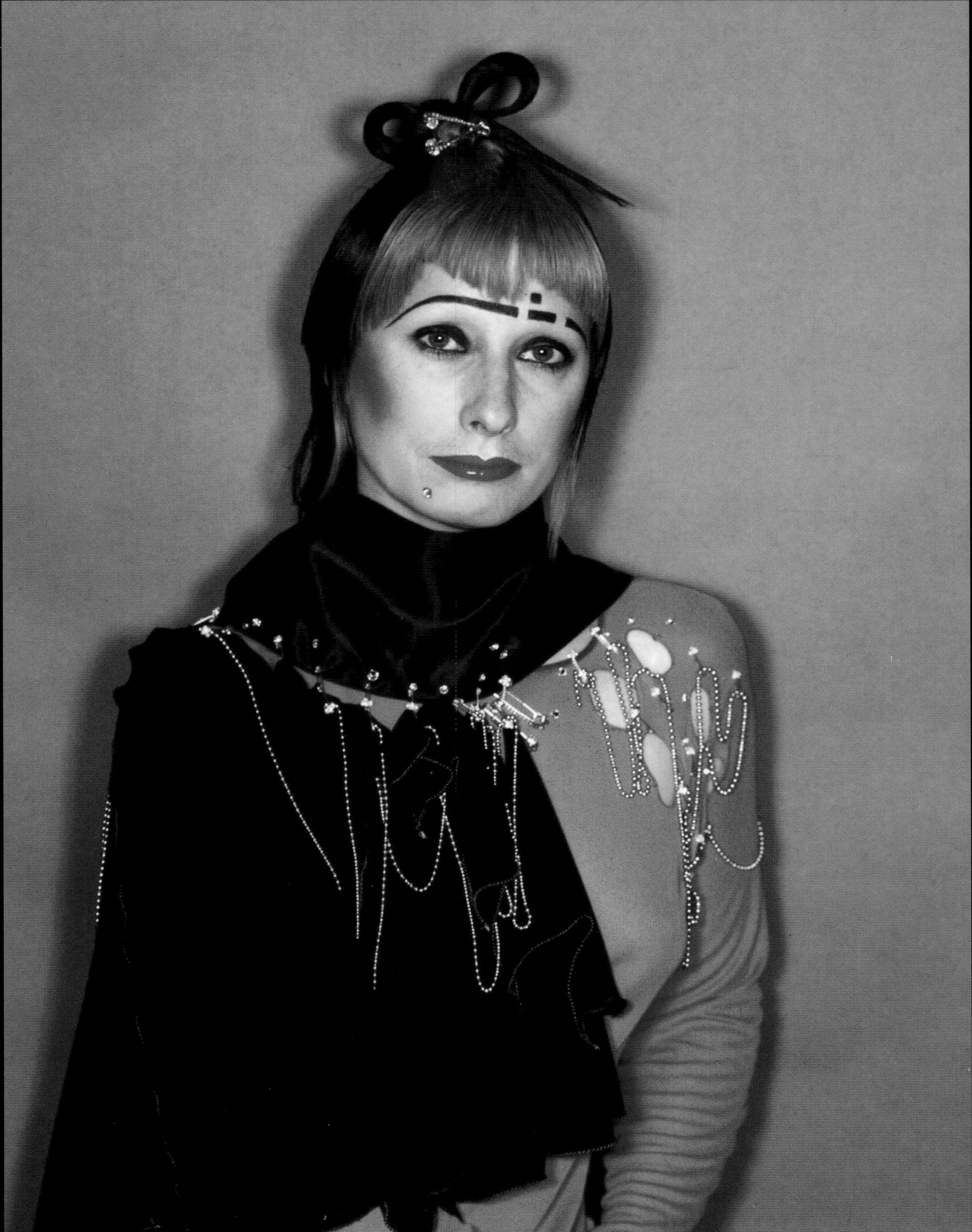

Zandra *is* the world of fashion

Andrew Logan

When I came to London from Peru in the '70s, Zandra was all anyone was talking about in fashion and I remember working with her designs back then. Her work was so unique. It is amazing that 25 years later I photographed her for UK Vogue alongside other fashion icons; and she still continues to inspire the new talent. Her work is still unique and instantly recognisable among contemporary designs. There are few designers who have that kind of longevity.

first & second   left to right
third & fourth   photographs by Robyn Beeche
fifth   photographs by Herbert Schultz
photograph by Robyn Beeche

Zandra's colourful ideas and equally colourful personality have made and will continue to make her an enduring presence.

Her work is whimsical and extraordinary. Her clothes are works of art and well made. Larry likes to see them hanging on the wall like you would hang a painting or display a sculpture.

Larry and Maj Hagman

"I'm a textile designer that couldn't find a job" she says, "and went into fashion by accident".

Zandra was convinced of three things: that her work should stand in comparison with that of the painters and sculptors; that there was more to life than designing fabrics for other people to cut about; and, most dramatic of all, that she herself was part of a canvas on which her visual ideas could be tried out: she would become a walking, talking research and development department.

Shortly after leaving the Royal College of Art, Zandra - with a Zee - realised that both she and her textile designs had too strong a personality to fit into someone else's fashions. She taught herself to make clothes the way she wanted then them to be, letting the textiles influence the shapes of the garments - creating prints, printing, designing clothes, pattern-making, cutting out dresses and hand-rolling edges all herself.

The influences on her work have ranged across the spectrum from the paintings of Kandinsky, Modigliani and Matisse, to Elizabethan costumes in the Victoria and Albert Museum, to a rock in the Australian outback, to the safety pins and bin liners of London Street Culture in the late 1970s. Whatever the visual stimulus, the resulting garments remain unmistakably Zandra. And it is this that is recognised wherever fashion is valued as both art and as design.

Christopher Frayling,

Without question, her dynamic personality and individuality are beyond the realms of most people's comprehension, giving her the right to be called an innovator of rare dimension.

Vidal Sassoon

right Freddie Mercury, 1974
photograph by Mick Rock, 2004

next pages British Vogue
photographs by Norman Parkinson,
model Jerry Hall, 1976

VOGUE'S OWN MOTOR SHOW

Zandra Rhodes satin sarong, Rover to match . . . Frilled sarong of pleated satin in whipped cream print, tendrils of rouleaux and gilded cords keeping body and soul together; to order from Zandra Rhodes. Elbeo tights. Gold heels, Manolo Blahnik, £28, at Zapata. Gold disc/bead earrings, £9, shell necklace, £45, Saint Laurent Rive Gauche

picture credits

FTM photography by Robyn Beeche,
assistant Jason Smith at the FTM photographic studio

We would like to thank the following for letting us use their
photography within this book;

Roman Alonzon, 100
Clive Arrowsmith, 5, 8, 11, 54, 78, 80, 82, 84, 85, 86, 89, 124, 125
Piers Atkinson, Cover
Richard Avedon, 135
David Bailey, 59, 90, 95, 110
Frank Bauer, 150
Robyn Beeche, 96, 115, 116, 117, 118, 119, 122, 123, 124, 126, 127, 128, 130,
132, 133, 138, 142, 143, 145, 146, 148, 149
Guy Bourdin, 74, 75, 76
Eric Bowman, 147
Henry Clarke, 45
Norman Eales, 38, 64
Lisa Eisner, 56, 100
Daniela Federici, 158
Joe Gaffney, 107, 120, 144
Ken Haydon, Back cover inside flap
Steve Hyatt, 140, 141
Bishin Jumonji, 73, 137
Art Kane, 42
Alex von Koettlitz, 18
Barry Lategan, 108, 112, 1113
David LaChapelle, 52
Jim Lee, 99
Caterine Milinaire, 40
Alix Malka, 105
Gity Monsef, 22, 23, 24, 25, 26, 27, 28, 29
Swapan Mukerjee, 67
Grant Mudford, 142
Norman Parkinson, 12, 92, 154, 155
Stan Ribton, 71
Mick Rock, www.mickrock.com, 153
Conrad Santavicca, 36
Francesco Scavullo, 102
Herbert Schultz, 149
Maurits Sillem, 151
Tim Street-Porter, 140
Simon Wheeler, Back cover
Yu-Kuang, 156

donors & lenders

157

Robyn Beeche (78/65)
Evangeline Bruce (70/23)
Valerie Cooper (79/124, 79/141)
Frances Diplock (74/47)
Martha Gafford (85/96)
Lady Iveagh (Z2)
Jeannie Jones (94/60)
Michaela Lawrence (74/50v)
Barbara Lazaroff (36/?)
Joan Agajanian Quinn (81/79, 81/87)
Sarah Holcroft on behalf of her mother Lady Rothermere (73/44)
Marjorie Rubin (85/102, 74/5c, Z6, 71/6)
Dasha Shenkman in the name of her mother Belle Shenkman (71/28)

All other garments on loan from the Zandra Rhodes Archives to the FTM.

contributors

Robyn Beeche an Australian photographer, worked in London from the mid-seventies until the end of the '80s, she now resides in India. Her photographic contribution to the 'Art of Zandra Rhodes' book forms the basis of the photographic archive at the Museum. She is also very well known for her fashion and extraordinary beauty photographs of the '80s for clients such as Vivienne Westwood, Bill Gibb, Yuki and Jasper Conran. A large selection of her work is held at the National Gallery of Australia.

At 31, **Robert de Niet** has worked for over 16 years as a graphic designer and typographer. His clients include BBC TV, Citi Bank, Diesel, M&C Saatchi, Stüssy, V&A, Virgin Mobile and Walt Disney. He is currently senior lecturer of Graphic Design: New Media at the Surrey Institute of Art & Design, and also lectures in graphics, fashion and fashion journalism.

Production designer **Michael Howells** brings a theatrical and historical twist to his film and fashion creations. His films include 'Bright Young Things', 'Shackleton', 'Emma' and the forthcoming 'Nanny McPhee'. From 1997 he designed spectacular sets for John Galliano and Christian Dior, which lead to other shows for Galliano's womenswear and menswear lines, as well as Christian Lacroix and Alexander McQueen. Howells has collaborated with photographers including Nick Knight, Mert & Marcus and Mario Testino on publications and campaigns as diverse as Vogue, Pop, Vanity Fair, Christian Dior and Louis Vuitton. Michael has also brought his unique vision to Comme des Garcons at Dover St Market, 'Towards Poetry' for the Royal Ballet and 'Derdemon' for the Staatsoper Berlin Company. He is currently working on a new ballet entitled 'Constant Speed' to celebrate Einstein's Centenary for the Rambert Ballet for 2005.

159

Gity Monsef is Creative Director of the Fashion and Textile Museum with a working relationship with Zandra Rhodes that spans almost ten years. She has been a key figure in the strategic and creative development of the Museum. She is lead curator of Zandra's retrospective A Life Long Love Affair with Textiles (Winter 2005) and curated the museum's successful opening exhibition My Favourite Dress (Spring 2003), Daisy de Villeneuve: Not You Again (Summer 2004), the museum's first photographic exhibition Love On The Rocks (Fall 2004). Gity was instrumental in bridging the gap between the museum and the community with the museums first community initiative project Stop, Drop and Listen! The Children's Magic Mural.

Dennis Nothdruft began his career in fashion as Zandra Rhodes' assistant in her California Studio, where he worked with her for fives years. He was an award-winning fashion teacher at FCC College in San Diego, winning Teacher of the Year two years running. He has since joined the team at Fashion and Textile Museum, where he has been developing the museum's education initiatives, as well as curating the exhibition Permanently in Fashion and co-curating Sampling the '70s and Not You Again by Daisy de Villeneuve with the FTM Exhibitions team.

Brenda Polan is a freelance journalist who specialises in fashion and design. She has worked for a wide range of publications including the Daily Mail, the Financial Times, The Guardian, The Independent, The Mail on Sunday, The Daily Telegraph and The Evening Standard as well as a variety of newspaper supplements (You, How To Spend It, Style, Night and Day) and glossy magazines (Tatler, World of Interiors, Elle, Red, Good Housekeeping). She also lectures in fashion journalism at the London College of Fashion and the Surrey Institute of Art & Design.

Ben Scholten trained at Arnhem Art College, The Netherlands, winning several International Fashion Awards, and has worked with Zandra since 1975 and is, together with her, responsible for the designing of the Zandra Rhodes collections and their realisation. He has also designed for the theatre and developed corporate uniforms for a number of companies. He regularly lectures to national and international colleges and universities about his work as a designer.

Kelly Osbourne
photograph by
Daniela Federici

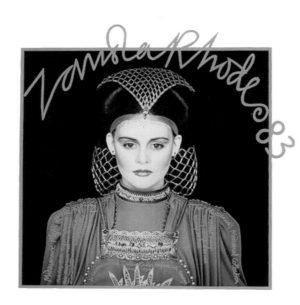